MARRY YOUR

Muse

MARRY YOUR

Muse

MAKING A LASTING COMMITMENT
TO YOUR CREATIVITY

A publication supported by
THE KERN FOUNDATION

Quest Books
Theosophical Publishing House

Wheaton, Illinois ♦ Chennai (Madras), India

The Theosophical Publishing House
P.O. Box 270
Wheaton, IL 60189-0270

A publication of the Theosophical Publishing House,
a department of the Theosophical Society in America

Cover and book design by Beth Hansen

Library of Congress Cataloging-in-Publication Data

Phillips, Jan.
        Marry your muse: making a lasting commitment to your creativity /
    Jan Phillips. — 1st Quest ed.
            p.   cm.
        ISBN 0-8356-0759-3
        1. Creative ability.   2. Creative ability—Problems, exercises, etc.
    3. Creation (Literary, artistic, etc.)   I. Title.
BF408.P47   1997
153.3'5—dc21   97-19472
                                                                              CIP

Grateful acknowledgment is made for persmission to reprint the following copyrighted material:

From the book *The Individual and the Nature of Mass Events, A Seth Book*, ©1995 Robert Butts.
Reprinted by permission of Amber-Allen Publishing, Inc., P.O. Box 6657, San Rafael, CA
94903. All rights reserved.

From *The Divine Milieu*, Teilhard de Chardin, HarperCollins Publishers.

Page 244: photograph by Irene Young

6   5   4   3   2   1   ★   97   98   99   00   01   02

Printed in the United States of America

Dedication

I dedicate this book to the memory of Susan O'Flaherty,
whose lightness and courage inspire us still.

Contents

Acknowledgments

I give thanks to the Source of All Creation and to my Muse, Rebecca, for the faith and fire it took to bring this book to life.

Also to my partner, Annie, thank you for believing in me, for reading each page and saying "Yes!" and for calling forth the light in the darkest of times;

To the artists who contributed your stories and work, thank you for taking time to pass on the stardust in the midst of all your other projects;

To Brenda Rosen at Quest Books, thank you for finding this book and making it happen; and to Jane Lawrence for your kind and careful editing;

To Hannelore Hahn, thank you for believing in your dream and starting the International Women's Writing Guild, a community I cherish and look to for hope;

And to the women in my first *Marry Your Muse* workshop at the International Women's Writing Guild Summer Conference at Skidmore College, I thank you for the circle of energy out of which this book swirled.

Introduction

This book is an exploration into possibility, an exercise in dissolving the line between the mundane and the mystical, the sacred and the secular. It begins with the assumption that we are all inherently creative and that we have only learned to think of ourselves as anything less than that. As much as this book is about doing, it is about undoing—undoing our self-doubt, undoing our fears of self-expression, undoing our illusions that creativity belongs to a chosen few. It celebrates not only the joy of creating, but also the joy of being re-created ourselves as we draw upon our depths and tap into our Source.

In the process of creating, we are attempting to transform one thing into another—our experience into words, our dreams into dance, our fears or fantasies into poems, songs, or plays. Once we start the work, a new energy arises as the piece takes on a life of its own, passing through us on its way to fullness. We become, then, not so much creators as collaborators with this form, this idea, this new life that seeks expression.

We shape it, we give it color and texture, we break it down into notes on a musical staff, but the melody, the power, the soul of the piece—this comes as a gift of spirit. And this, to me, is the sacredness of creativity—this bubbling up of newness from the space within where our emptiness is home to All That Is.

I have read that all life and energy are generated from the union of two polar opposites. Before thought is born, two hemispheres of the brain must combine forces. Perhaps too before art is created, the mortal on some level must merge with the Divine, opening up to the essence of what seeks to be created. Our creations, then, would become manifestations of divine union, much as our bodies are manifestations of divine thought. If all parts seek the whole, and we in our mortality seek the Divine, perhaps divinity finds its rapture in merging with the mortal.

Throughout the centuries, the Muse, the goddess of creativity, has been seen as an angel hovering over the shoulder of the artist at work. We see her outside ourselves as we have been taught to see God, as a force transcendent, above and beyond us. But imagine that she is immanent, within us, of us. Imagine that spirit is seeking to create through us, to regenerate itself into this culture, word waiting to be made flesh through our creative expressions. Imagine the Muse ever poised, constantly ready to cocreate, full of grace and awesome beauty. Imagine yourself the vessel of transmission, the one chosen to birth the sacred, in word, song, clay, image, or dance.

Do not doubt that you are born to create. Do not believe for a minute that the realm of art belongs only to others. Do not believe what you have been told or think you heard: that you are incapable, unimaginative, not artistic. This is blasphemous—it denies the potential to create, which is your birthright. If you have believed these things and woven your garment from doubt and fear, disrobe and look within. Find what brings you joy and go there. That is your place to create, to move with the spirit, for the Muse lingers near the home of your joy.

There is no absolute truth about the Muse or the creative process. Creativity is of the inner realm. Each of us becomes our own expert. In our seeking, we find what was never lost. In our creating, we ourselves are created, added to, enlightened. What matters is the movement, the union with spirit, that subtle drive that wakes us from our sleep, takes us from our dreams, and invites us to become the dream expressed.

PART ONE

Committing to the Creative Journey

Whenever I talk to groups of people about creativity, they always share long lists of reasons why they aren't being as creative as they want to be. No time, no space to work in, no privacy in their lives; and deeper, more troublesome issues like feeling isolated, not believing in the value of their work, doubting their abilities in the face of rejection.

Committing to our creativity is an act of faith, a promise that we will keep at it despite our fears and failings and despite whatever obstacles we find in our paths. It is a promise to believe in ourselves, to honor the creative process, and to open our lives to the gifts of the Muse.

This section of the book is based on a prayer of commitment, "The Artist's Creed," and its intention is to keep us mindful of the sacredness of our work and the value of our creations.

The Artist's Creed

*I believe I am worth the time it takes to create
whatever I feel called to create.*

*I believe that my work is worthy of its own space,
which is worthy of the name Sacred.*

*I believe that, when I enter this space, I have the right
to work in silence, uninterrupted, for as long as I choose.*

*I believe that the moment I open myself to the gifts of the Muse,
I open myself to the Source of All Creation
and become One with the Mother of Life Itself.*

*I believe that my work is joyful, useful, and constantly changing,
flowing through me like a river with no beginning and no end.*

*I believe that what it is I am called to do
will make itself known when I have made myself ready.*

*I believe that the time I spend creating my art
is as precious as the time I spend giving to others.*

*I believe that what truly matters in the making of art is
not what the final piece looks like or sounds like,
not what it is worth or not worth, but what newness gets added
to the universe in the process of the piece itself becoming.*

*I believe that I am not alone in my attempts to create,
and that once I begin the work, settle into the strangeness,
the words will take shape, the form find life, and the spirit take flight.*

*I believe that as the Muse gives to me,
so does she deserve from me:
faith, mindfulness, and enduring commitment.*

I believe I am worth the time it takes

to create whatever I feel called to create.

You Are Worth the Time

We have a funny concept of time in this culture. We revere it as we revere money, yet we rarely spend any of it on ourselves. We complain that we can't make what time we have go around, yet day after day we spend our allotment doing things we don't really want to be doing.

The other day I was talking with an artist whose full-time job left her little time to devote to her fine art projects. When I asked what she would like to be working on, she said she was so stressed out she couldn't even imagine what she would do if she had the time. The voice that once called her to creative work is being drowned out by the din of the daily grind, and I suspect a day will come when she forgets she ever heard it.

In *The Tibetan Book of Living and Dying*, Buddhist meditation master Sogyal Rinpoche writes of our tendency to fill up our whole lives with petty projects and never get to the real questions, like Why are we here? and What are we doing with our lives? He calls it "active laziness" and describes both Eastern and Western manifestations of it. In the East, it consists of lounging around all day in the sun, drinking tea, gossiping with friends, and listening to music blaring on the radio. In the West, he writes, it consists of "cramming our lives with compulsive activity, so that there is no time at all to confront the real issues."

Other than about the weather, at least here in the northeast, there is no complaint as constant as the one about time. It used to be that one couple could arrange a dinner date with another couple by deciding on an evening and making a single phone call. These days it's four people

As I look back on what I have written, I can see that the very persons who have taken away my time are those who have given me something to say.
—Katherine Paterson

I couldn't find anything that truly reflected what I thought was my reality and the reality of other women my age. Since I couldn't find it, the only responsible recourse was to write some myself.
—Ntozake Shange

checking their Day-Timers, one fax after another of possible dates weeks into the future, then endless games of phone tag to nail down a designated evening.

When it comes to making time for creative projects—projects that are fun, imaginative, life affirming, mood altering, and spiritually nourishing—we are hard pressed to justify our choices. Time has become a synonym for money in this culture, and the use of it is often measured by its profit potential. If the work makes money, it is time well spent. If the work is not profitable, it is a waste of our time.

We have come to define ourselves by what we do to pay the bills. The question "What do you do?" generally means "How do you make your living?" It rarely has anything to do with the calling in one's heart or the time we spend on work that has nothing to do with money. In Corita Kent's book, *Learning by Heart*, she writes that in Balinese culture, "when you ask a person what he does, he will proudly answer that he is a mask maker or a dancer. And if you persist and ask again, No, I mean how do you get your rice? He loses interest, his voice drops, and he may turn away, deciding this is a pretty boring conversation. 'Oh that,' he will say."

Having been raised in a country where time equals money and profits are more safeguarded than the welfare of people, I was surprised to experience an environment where people came first. It was in southern India at a Gandhian ashram. The community was in the process of building a new barn. Eighty people had gathered to help out. We met at the edge of a stream, about a quarter of a mile from the building site. Though no one in particular issued any orders, the group quietly formed into a long line from the stream, up a hill, up a ladder against a small cliff, through a meadow and to the site of the new barn, where young women were hauling rocks on their heads for the foundation. It was monsoon season. Though it was still early morning the temperature was already 100 degrees and the air was heavy with humidity.

Our job was to pass tin bowls of sand, stones, and water from the stream to be used as mortar. From one person to the other, hand to hand, the bowls were passed along the snaking line. Hour after hot, heavy hour went by, yet not one person complained. Women wrapped in six yards of sari were giggling and gossiping as they passed the bowls

Poetry and mysticism both derive from a common source, the ground or depth of the soul, where the Mystery of Being is experienced.
—Bede Griffiths

Our lives seem to live us, to possess their own bizarre momentum, to carry us away; in the end we feel we have no choice or control over them.
—Sogyal Rinpoche

Just as you began to feel that you could make good use of time, there was no time left to you.
—Lisa Alther

effortlessly. Teenage boys, gracing the ladder on every third rung, outdid each other in showy panache. By midmorning, I was soaking wet and losing steam. At one point, I squinted into the wavy heat and scanned the landscape for signs of relief. My eyes hit on two tractors in a nearby meadow. Then I spotted two idle carts on the side of the road. Moments later, a group of ashram kids passed by leading a team of oxen to the river. It suddenly appeared ridiculous that all this people power was being used to pass bowls of mortar when the job could get done much more efficiently using oxen, tractors, and carts.

"This is stupid!" I shouted to Nayan Bala, an English-speaking woman from Delhi who stood next to me in line. "We've got forty people here wasting a whole morning in this heat, passing buckets like there's no tomorrow. Why don't we hook up the carts to those tractors and oxen and let them do the dirty work in half the time? Don't you know time is money?"

I knew, even as those final words tumbled out of my mouth, that every one of them was a mistake, but they were traveling too fast to stop. Nayan Bala put her bucket down and walked over to my side. Gently, she put her hand on my sweaty arm and whispered in my ear, "These people are proud to be building this barn with their own hands. One day they will bring their children and grandchildren here and tell them how they helped build it, rock by rock. Perhaps you have more to learn about India if you think this is a waste of time."

I was ashamed of myself, ashamed of ever buying into the time-is-money myth and ashamed of criticizing a process that was more about people than profit or time. It wasn't just India I had more to learn about. It was the whole notion of time, of the time it takes to create, and of how such time can never be wasted.

In the process of creating, time is one of the essential ingredients. If art is a result of the encounter between Muse and artist, then time is the medium of the relationship. Time is what we bring as an offering, a sign of our commitment. Without this, there is no creating.

Whatever we attempt to create, if we come to the work with the intention of producing something original, something that only we could make given who we are and what we have experienced, then we are engaging in an artistic activity that is worthy of whatever time it takes.

Making time for creative work is like making time for prayer. It is a

Art can only be truly art by presenting an adequate outward symbol of some fact in the interior life.
—*Margaret Fuller*

What was any art but an effort to make a sheath, a mold in which to imprison for a moment the shining, elusive element which is life itself—life hurrying past us and running away, too strong to stop, too sweet to lose?
—*Willa Cather*

To survive we must begin to know sacredness. The pace at which most of us live prevents this.
—*Chrystos*

The greatest productions of art, whether painting, music, sculpture or poetry, have invariably this quality—something approaching the work of God.

—D. T. Suzuki

I am a dancer. I believe that we learn by practice. Whether it means to learn to dance by practicing dancing or to learn to live by practicing living, the principles are the same. In each it is the performance of a dedicated precise set of acts, physical or intellectual, from which come shape of achievement, a sense of one's being, a satisfaction of spirit. One becomes in some area an athlete of God.

—Martha Graham

holistic activity, involving the visible and invisible, the known and unknown. To create is to make something whole from the pieces of our lives and, in the process, to become more whole ourselves, seeing with more clarity each of those pieces, understanding where they fit, how they matter. It is a healing act, a leave-taking from the chaos as one moves from the choppy surface toward the stillness of the center.

To be an artist it is not necessary to make a living from our creations. Nor is it necessary to have work hanging in fine museums or the praise of critics. It is not necessary that we are published or that famous people own our work. To be an artist it *is* necessary to live with our eyes wide open, to breathe in the colors of mountain and sky, to know the sound of leaves rustling, the smell of snow, the texture of bark. It is necessary to rub our hands all over life, to sing when and where we want, to take in every detail, and to jump when we get to the edge of the cliff. To be an artist is to notice every beautiful and tragic thing, to cry freely, to collect experience and shape it into forms that others can share.

It is not to whine about not having time, but to be creative with every moment. To be an artist is not to wait for others to define us, but to define ourselves, claim our lives, create for love, not money. It is to know the joy of collaboration with the Muse, to become familiar with the magic of how it works: we hear a voice, feel a nudge, and start the work. We keep on, not knowing where we're going, and some clues come, and then they don't, and we keep on, and one day it is finished and we know it is ours but not ours alone, so we offer thanks and bow our heads. This is what is to be an artist.

Our cities and towns are full of poets, playwrights, composers, and painters who drive buses, work in offices, wait on tables to pay the rent. Few of us are paid much for our creative work, so we squeeze it into the hours we have left after working other jobs. We write our novels in the wee hours of the morning, work in our darkrooms through the night, write poetry on subway cars, finish essays in waiting rooms and parking lots. We rarely think of ourselves as artists, though it is our creative work that brings us to life, feeds our spirits, and sees us through the dark. We may feel alone, but we are *not* alone. There are hundreds, thousands in the night doing as we do, trading this sacred time for the bliss of creating.

There are a lot of things we don't have in life, but time is not one of them. Time is all we have. One lifetime under this name to produce a body of work that says, "This is how I saw the world." Your work is worthy of whatever time it takes.

Dear Muse,

I call your name.
Will you come to my side
and stir the visions that lie within?
If I offer my time, my hands,
my deepest desire
to make a thing that matters,
will you help make a whole
from the pieces I've gathered?

I long to create
but am hushed by doubt,
silenced by fear
that I haven't the wisdom or wherewithal
to bring to art what art demands.

Will you come to my side
and whisper what's true
when I forget what gifts I have to give?
When I think my words have nothing to add,
will you help me remember
what I've learned from others
who thought the same
but dared to speak?

O Muse, I need you,
I call out your name.
Will you please call mine,
call me back,
call me home.

Dear Child,

Your name is on the breeze
blowing ever round you
and you are wrapped in the light
though your eyes are closed.

You have forgotten
and must once again remember:
the way to create
is to let what is in you
come forth as it will.

You give your time to doubt and fear
when no value comes of that.
Better to give time to the journey inward,
to that voice that needs you
to sound its truth.

Turn your ear
to the stories that call you,
the memories that linger
and wait for reclaiming.

Your desire to create
is the calling of these tales.
It is the tales that stir you,
the tales that hold all the words
you will ever need.
Just listen now and remember.

I believe that my work is worthy of its own space,

which is worthy of the name Sacred.

Your Work Is Worthy

As important as time is to the creative process, so too is the space in which we work. If we are committed to collaborating with the Muse, then we must set the stage for the piece to unfold. It may not be that we have a studio or a whole room to devote to our art. It is more likely that we will carve out of a larger space something smaller, defined as sacred by what is missing as much as by what is present.

To create the sacred space, we start from nothing. We define its parameters, clear it of accoutrements, and bless the emptiness. Then we bring to the space only that which leads us into harmony with our own center, fortifies us, reflects our intention, reminds us of the reason we are there. Our sacred space should be defined in such a way that everything in it becomes a metaphor for the journey out of the secular realm and into the spiritual, where we disengage from the limits of time and temporal concerns.

This is a place where our consciousness is transformed, where we light the candle and announce our presence to the Muse. This is where we say, "I have come to do the work, and all my attention is upon it." Here we open ourselves to the joy and mystery of creation itself. It is within this sacred space that we unite with the One we have longed for, reaching no longer but reveling in the found.

Sacred space is a playground for the soul. It is a place of refuge and newness, a place where we ourselves define the limits or lack of them. Here we set out on a journey of our own making to a destination that is finally determined by the journey itself. It is a place of rendezvous with the great love of our lives; a secret, sacred meeting ground where life is

Women have always been poor, not for two hundred years merely, but from the beginning of time. . . . Women, then, have not had a dog's chance of writing poetry. That's why I have laid so much stress on money and a room of one's own.
—Virginia Woolf

When half-gods go, the gods arrive.
—Ralph Waldo Emerson

conceived, renewed, embraced, and enchanted.

The sacred space is made holy by the purity of our intention. The Muse, as always, awaits us and the liaison is vitalized by our energy and attention. When we are there, we are wholly present, leaning into possibility, and bringing to the table both our fullness and our emptiness.

We come with open arms, ready to make magic with the Muse and to break through any barriers that keep us separate. As we welcome her and invite her assistance, she enters the space and takes her place. It is our part, then, to open to her gifts, follow her lead, and see where she takes us. Each of us will do this in our own way, and we need no direction except to listen very carefully.

One may do this in total silence while another chooses a background of music. One may sit before a blank page in an open notebook; another before a canvas with a palette of fresh paint. We need our tools handy for she will be using them, guiding us, pushing like a gentle wind at our back while we walk toward the new and yet-to-be-created.

In 1981, I left my home in Hawaii and headed for the hills of Oregon to join a group of women who were putting together a journal of feminist photography. Ruth and Jean Mountaingrove had been publishing *Womanspirit* magazine from this location for years, and I was looking forward to meeting them, to spending some time in a rural environment, and to contributing what I could as a writer and photographer.

I hitchhiked up from Berkeley and had a four-mile walk from the interstate exit where my ride left me off. Ruth and Jean lived on top of a mountain near Sunny Valley. When I arrived, hot and sweaty, I was warmly welcomed by the two of them, along with Tee Corinne and Caroline Overman, all editors of the forthcoming *Blatant Image*.

Although I had never been introduced to the concept of sacred spaces, when Jean walked me up the path toward my cabin, she pointed out several sacred spaces she and others had landscaped in the woods. Sometimes there would be just a stump surrounded by a circle of evergreen boughs, sometimes a chair under an arbor, sometimes just feathers and ribbons strung from branches. "Sacred spaces are important things," said Jean. "You always need at least one, but you can never have too many."

Poetry is the voice of the soul.
—*Carolyn Forche*

Your sacred space is where you can find yourself again and again.
—*Joseph Campbell*

One does not impose one's will on a space. One listens.
—*Louis Kahn*

In oneself lies the whole world, and if you know how to look and learn, then the door is there and the key is in your hand. Nobody on earth can give you either that key or the door to open, except yourself.
—*Krishnamurti*

The cabin I was to live in was about twelve by sixteen feet with two windows facing the woods. There was no electricity, but there was a small potbellied stove for wood burning and a kerosene lamp for nighttime reading and writing. The bed was a wooden plank covered with a piece of foam, and beside it was a small desk that looked like something Abe Lincoln might have used.

We worked every morning from nine till twelve, sorting through hundreds of photographs submitted by women from across the country. We broke for lunch from noon until three, then continued working. I spent a lot of time in my tiny cabin, the first room of my own in a long time, as I had been sharing a house with five women in Honolulu. It took awhile to find my stride in a place with no bathrooms, no electricity, and none of the usual comforts of home, but once I became acclimated, I never wanted to leave. That little cabin was all I needed—a small bed, a small desk, a stove for warmth, a light for reading, and no distractions other than an occasional moth or curious chipmunk.

The pace was slow and deliberate, set by the elders, Ruth and Jean, who had a keen sense of what to honor. A good part of the afternoon was taken for solitude. Some gardened, some slept, some wrote, some read. Then each of us returned to the group fully energized and eager to work.

To me, it was like heaven being up there in the mountains, working at a pace that seemed to match the body's rhythms, and having those little woodsy sacred spaces, that little wooden hermitage, and all those paths linking one with the other. Had I consciously tried to follow my bliss, this is the place it would have taken me.

Now I live in an urban environment with a pace as frantic as any other city's. No one has gone about the neighborhood creating sacred spaces. No one has designed a midday break into the workday for recollection or rest. It is push, push, push, produce, produce, produce, and we all respond as if this were natural.

I have no chipmunks visiting my workplace. No birds chirp outside the window. I don't even *have* a window in the office where I work as a consultant a few days a week. So while I am there, it is up to me to remember to set a pace that honors what's important. It is up to me to make wherever I am a sacred space, to come mindfully to my tasks, calmly to the chaos.

Since many of us do not have a room of our own, it is important that

The key is what is within the artist. The artist can only paint what she or he is about.
—Lee Kramer

There is nothing so secular that it cannot be sacred, and that is one of the deepest messages of the Incarnation.
—Madeleine L'Engle

Go, not knowing where; bring, not knowing what; the path is long, the way unknown; the hero knows not how to arrive there by himself.
—Russian fairy tale

All that is true, by whomsoever it has been said, has its origin in the Spirit.
—Thomas Aquinas

we each determine how to make a space in our lives where we can work in peace and without distraction. To create, if only within our own minds, a space for the inner work that creativity demands, into which no one can enter and no noise can penetrate. If we lack physical space, we need to create a sacred space of consciousness, where we leave confusion behind and rest our mind in the wisdom mind of the Muse. We are ready, then, to converse with her, to ask our questions, and to open ourselves to the work taking shape.

It is not that we come without ideas, but that we listen in a different way, a deeper way, to the voice within. We listen for the soul of the thing we are about to create and come to a sense of the whole of it—not necessarily to have an image of it in our minds, but to have sense of its fullness, to know the root of it, so that when we start to build, we may begin there, at its real core.

We want to feel the pulse of the poem before we write the first word, sense its resonance in our beings, feel the tug of its urgency. We want to remember that this thing already has life, is an essence waiting to be shaped, colored, and textured by the touch of our hands, the choice of our words. As it passes through us, it will change us as surely as waves change the rocks they break across each day.

To allow creation to occur within us is to expose ourselves to an ever-changing flow of truth and beauty. It is to practice the discipline of openness, to learn to trust, to dare to risk the surprises that emerge as our work evolves.

Creative work is a means of finding ourselves and of providing ways for others to find themselves as well. Nancy Mairs writes in *Voice Lessons*, "Our stories utter one another. . . . If I do my job, the books I write vanish before your eyes. I invite you into the house of my past, and the threshold you cross leads you into your own."

This is the universality of art. This is its power and its reach—that what we create can be a bridge of understanding, can help us to perceive with more compassion the experience of another's perspective. It is only right, then, that work of this nature should have a space of its own.

Dear Muse,

Today I have made
a space for you,
I call it sacred
and ask you in.
A white candle burns
to the sound of empty,
a feather before it,
a shell behind.

Like a Shinto priest
ringing bells to the gods
to wake them up and
summon their help,
I call for you
with fire and drum.
O come, come near,
come be with me.

Come sing your knowing
to the ears of my wonder,
come bring your dawn
to the arms of my dark.
Come be the thought
that gets shaped into word,
O come, with the warm wet
breath of birth.

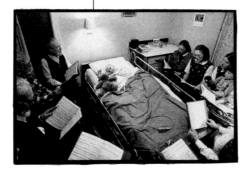

Dear Child,

It is good to remember
that all ground is sacred
where life is honored
and that you can build a temple
in the space between your eyes.

Remember as well,
when you light the candle
and call out my name,
that I am near you every moment
only waiting for your wanting
and the stirring of your heart.

It is not for me
you need make this space,
but for you yourself
to claim such a thing,
a place to be open
to your deeper knowing,
to hear the voice of your soul,
the words of its Wisdom.

I believe that, when I enter this space, I have the right

to work in silence, uninterrupted, for as long as I choose.

You Have the Right

When I was in the novitiate, I lived at the Motherhouse in community with four hundred sisters. Our days were filled from morning till evening with prayers, meals, housework, laundry, classes, recreation, study, and sleep. Since prayers took a good portion of the day, much of our time was spent in chapel.

As part of our training, we were required to visit the chapel regularly, for morning and evening meditations, communal prayers and Stations of the Cross. It was a beautiful sanctuary with a towering mosaic backdrop of softly-hued imported granite. The mosaic depicted an image of the resurrected Christ in a white robe, standing with his arms outstretched and a gentle, loving look on his face. It had the distinction of being the largest stone mosaic in the country, and it was the most exquisite sanctuary I had ever seen. A pearl-gray marble altar in the form of a chalice cast its reflection across the shiny marble floor, and rainbow light filtered through the stained-glass windows, dancing over rows of light-oak pews.

At any time of day or night, one would find older sisters in traditional habits, stooped in their seats, prayer books in hand, lost in communion with their Great Beloved. I loved the sight of them and would often go to the choir loft and peer down at them, a witness to their commitment, to this love affair with the Unseen. They came frequently for visits and often stayed for hours at a time, hunched over, sometimes sleeping, sometimes fingering their beads, but more often than not, simply being in the Presence. As months went on and I matured in my own spiritual practice, I grew to understand what they found there and

We receive the light, then we impart it. Thus we repair the world.
—Kabbalah

Once we recognize what it is we are feeling, once we recognize we can feel deeply, love deeply, can feel joy, then we will demand that all parts of our lives produce that kind of joy.
—Audre Lorde

why they kept returning. I found the richness for myself, discovered the joy of this communion and the feel of its mystery.

As much as I loved the community events when we gathered together for play and recreation, so I loved our community prayers—the morning lauds and evening vespers when we brought the psalms to life, our voices calling out those soulful prayers, sisters on one side beginning the verse, sisters on the other side responding. It moved me like nothing else, this kind of sharing and focus of attention. There was an incredible energy that rose up in the room as four hundred voices became one, and I felt it every day, twice a day, so proud, so humbled to be part of it.

That room was filled with a kind of power I have never been able to describe, and the energy never left. I could sense it, breathe it in, any time of day or night. It was space made sacred by our intention and love, and I was drawn to it, as were those seniors who in their final, frail years still came to the altar as youthful virgins, full of innocence and passion.

The chapel was a sacred space for anyone who wanted one. It was ready-made—the candle always burning, the quiet always there. In my years at the Motherhouse, I came to rely on that space for the silence it offered and the privilege of uninterrupted solitude. It was one of the sweetest blessings of that lifestyle.

When I left the community, it was one of the things I missed most, for in the secular world there were few places one could go for this kind of solitude. I had to create an alternative chapel, devise other means to achieve that privacy and space for spiritual intimacy. I had to invent new parameters in my relationships with people, letting them know that there were times I needed to be alone and uninterrupted.

As I began to work on projects that called for focus and creative attention, I experienced the same need—to be totally alone when I entered the space I had defined as sacred. I was always living in households with other people, and it seemed to take forever for them to understand this need. Despite the fact that my door was shut, meditation music was playing, or incense was burning, housemates would still knock on my door to call me to the phone. Limits were tested by children, parents, and friends, all wondering how I could really put my personal or creative life ahead of them and their pressing needs.

To participate requires self-discipline and trust and courage, because this business of becoming conscious, of being a writer, is ultimately about asking yourself "How alive am I willing to be?"
—*Anne Lamott*

There is no need for temples; no need for complicated philosophy. Our own brain, our own heart is our temple; my philosophy is kindness.
—*The Dalai Lama*

A strong woman is a woman who loves strongly and weeps strongly and is strongly terrified and has strong needs.
—*Marge Piercy*

I went back and forth between feeling angry at their lack of understanding and feeling selfish for wanting a solitude I didn't deserve. After all, I was just writing or praying or sitting still as hundreds of thoughts raced through my brain. It was not as if I were perfecting some serum that would cure cancer or writing a novel for the best-seller list. It was just me working on my projects, but I called on the Holy Spirit for every one. Somehow that made it feel like prayer, deserving of quiet and my complete attention.

Over the years, I have come to appreciate the necessity of this solitude and make my requests with more confidence and ease. When I hear others say how hard it is for them to find any solitude in their lives, I flash back to my years of struggle with it, to the constant conversations I had with myself about whether I was worth it, whether my work was important enough to deserve being placed above the needs of others, and to the embarrassment I often felt when others failed to understand my need for prayer and aloneness.

In order to create the kind of art I wish to create, art that lends some light to the darkness, that makes a contribution beyond color and texture, sound, and form, I need to step aside from the chaos of daily life and open channels to a higher frequency, tuning in to the language of spirit, the voice of the Muse.

In attempting to collaborate with the unknown, to experience the wholeness of which I am part and manifest it in a tangible form, I am attempting a kind of alchemy which demands, as a first step, a journey inward.

It is a journey in the sense of movement toward, a journey of intention, of changing consciousness as I move from the state of being separate to the state of being with. Once I have traveled to the point where I am mindful of my oneness with spirit, then I am open to its energy, ready to create and to bring new life into being.

I think of this event as a sacrament and attend to it as I would any ritual of transformation. Aside from the solitude and defined space, I use whatever tools I need to maintain my focus as I make the shift from fragment to whole. I always light the candle as a sign of my intention and the beginning of my journey. There are incense and images to remind me of what I need to be mindful. Sometimes I play music that has the feel of a journey, the sound of the heavens. Then I close my

An inner reality is equally important to an outer reality.
—Gloria Steinem

Everything is gestation, then bringing forth.
—Rainer Maria Rilke

Art is not cozy and it is not mocked. Art tells the only truth that ultimately matters. It is the light by which human beings can be mended.
—Iris Murdoch

Poetry is the deification of reality.
—Edith Sitwell

eyes, open my heart, and believe myself forward, from the edge to the center.

It is an act of faith, different perhaps from the ones made by the elder sisters in the Motherhouse chapel, but equal in fervor, intent, and commitment. On some level, we are all artists, sharing the medium of life itself. Every day we add something new to the universe, bringing our human energy to the cosmic canvas. It is good to consider what we are contributing, good to do it intentionally, with the grandest of gestures, for this is our one brief chance to make a difference.

Consider your right to silence, to sacred space, and to the time it takes to prepare your gifts. You are as worthy of these as we are worthy of your greatness. So let it be.

Dear Spirit of All Creation,

I honor your presence and come in gratitude for all you've given. I love to be with you and cherish this communion. I long for my time with you, for this kind of attentiveness and solitude, though it is hard to claim in this busy world. So many voices call me here and there. So many distractions take me from this work, as if there is something more important I should be doing. I know I am meant to be here, creating with you, making something that speaks of my soul and brings forth some light that I can offer the world. The world is getting darker. I forget myself why I am here. I get confused, lose my balance, start believing in the illusions of this world—that I should have *more instead of* be *more. I worry that I have nothing to say that is worthwhile. I fear that nothing will come of all these hours and that what I offer will be rejected and scorned. I am afraid as often as I am not. Who am I to create? My voice is no more special than others'. Please guide me. Help me remember that this time with you is precious, that I learn from it, find myself, and help myself grow.*

Spirituality does not thrive in a vacuum: love, the fruit of the spirit, cannot help speaking in a prophetic voice, cannot help asserting itself in prophetic deeds. In the words of women, we come to understand that there is no such thing as individual redemption, that wholeness in our lives is inevitably tied to the well-being of the rest of creation.

—Marilyn Sewell

Dear Child,

    All these distractions and fears are part of your world. It does not serve you to deny them, but neither does it serve to give in to them. Do not be concerned with what you have to say and how it will be received. That is not what matters. What is important is for you to speak whatever voice you hear within. That is your only calling. Forget what others may say about it and think of those who may need your words as you have needed the words of others to help you on your way.

    Remember how you have been moved by the creations of others. Remember what joy, what cleansing insights, what surges of passion and hope they have stirred. What if the creators of those works had given in to their fears? What if all artists listened to the voice that denounces their gifts? What do you think propelled them on in the face of doubt? It is the same force that moves you—the force of divine beauty seeking expression in human form. You have come to experience the gift of humanity and to add to it what only you can add. This is not a burden, but a gift and a privilege. What you create as you render your experience into new forms will be a pathway home to your deeper self. As you create, you will grow in wisdom, connect what you know with what you dream, what you have felt with what you have faith in. As you pull from the mind and draw on the spirit, you will find new life breathed through you, breathed into the work that is before you. And this newness is the force of life itself, continuing through you, blessing you as it passes and becomes itself.

I believe that the moment I open myself to the gifts of the Muse,

I open myself to the Source of All Creation

and become One with the Mother of Life Itself.

Becoming One with Life

Every time I pass by one of those 3-D posters or cards in a shop, no matter how rushed I am, I have to stop for a short trip into that dimension. I have to put my nose up against that piece of art, move it back and forth in front of my eyes, stare into it as I would into a mirror, only not grasping visually at the surface, but looking through it, seeking not the image before me, but the thing beneath the image. Seeing not just one part, but the whole of the piece. It is a kind of looking that requires letting go of the ordinary to find the extraordinary. It is a looking *into* more than a looking *at*.

It's not that what I find when I finally get the right gaze is so exciting. So far the images have been quite mundane. The thrill comes in the shift that occurs when I finally see what's beneath the surface. Beneath this blur of colors and patterns with no apparent meaning or order, there is something to be found. Recognizable forms leap out of the background as I fix my gaze and deny distraction. Something new becomes available to me with a slight change in focus and avowed attention.

Standing there in that store, surrounded by shoppers rushing here and there, I'm reminded by something as simple as a poster of seven unicorns that I have access to other dimensions. What I see is never all there is. 3-D art jars my memory. It brings me back to a keener, different sense of seeing, and when I walk away from the poster or put down the card, I look around the room with an altered eye. I imagine whole other activities occurring beyond my sight. Though I cannot see what lingers

For me a true poem is on the way when I begin to feel haunted, when it seems as if I were being asked an inescapable question by an angel with whom I must wrestle to get at the answer.
—May Sarton

beyond my limited vision, I imagine spirits hovering, angels' arms resting on our shoulders, waves of energy passing from one being to another, colorful auras bouncing off every shopper. Whether any of this is true is beyond my knowing, but so too were those seven unicorns beyond my seeing when I first looked only on the surface.

In the matter of creativity, things seem much the same. I bring to the table what gifts I have as well as all my human limitations. I bring my fears, my doubts, my openness, my desire to be of service, and I hope that in the process of creating, some shift will occur that transforms the ordinary into the extraordinary.

In my ritual, I call on the Muse and acknowledge her presence. My prayer is not that she come to my ground, but that I reach hers—that I leave behind whatever thoughts and doubts I have that keep us separate and move into the experience of our oneness, feel the joy of it, speak the truth of it, and infuse my work with its energy. Once I open myself to the source and make of the work a prayerful gesture, I feel neither so alone nor so bound by my limitations. Instead of the fear of not being good enough, there is a sense of wonder about how this work will come out, what shape these thoughts will take as they move from mind through spirit to a form tangible enough to be held by another. I do not mind that some will find my work troublesome, for I am not writing to please or satisfy, but to express what I find deep within when I move to the center and shift my gaze.

Last winter, during of one of the worst blizzards of the season, I found myself on the on-ramp to a freeway with a thirty-mile commute ahead of me. It was already dark and the snow was pounding against my windshield like artillery bullets. There were no cars ahead offering the comforting glow of taillights to follow, and I could barely discern the road from the shoulder. I gripped the steering wheel so tightly my knuckles bulged like a mountain range through the soft leather of my gloves. Afraid to take my eyes of the road for a second, I fumbled around with half the knobs on the dashboard before I found the one to silence the radio. There could be no noise now—not at this juncture of life and death. I needed absolute concentration to maneuver my way out of this dark and terrifying danger.

I drove at twenty miles per hour, my nose only inches from the steering wheel. Hunched over in fear and focused alertness, I headed

Masterpieces are not single and solitary births; they are the outcome of many years of thinking in common, of thinking by the body of the people, so that the experience of the mass is behind the single voice.
—Virginia Woolf

I've been absolutely terrified every moment of my life and I've never let it keep me from doing a single thing I wanted to do.
—Georgia O'Keeffe

The tragic and fearful character of our times is not something from which we can detach ourselves; we are in it, as fish in the sea.
—Denise Levertov

straight into the storm as it whirled around me like a fierce tornado. There was nothing ahead but a raging swirl of white against a pitch black sky.

"Oh, my God," I prayed out loud, puffing small clouds of warm breath into the chilly air. "Please let me get through this alive."

No, I thought, *that's not good enough; I need to be more specific.* It wasn't just staying alive I wanted. It was a sense of safety, some relief from this swelling fear.

"OK, God, take the wheel. Get me home safe, OK?"

Now I was reverting to an eight-year-old Catholic who counted on the man with the beard to somehow materialize and work a miracle. That thought always pops up in an emergency, but I knew I had to go deeper than that. I couldn't be thinking of something outside of me. I had to focus every bit of attention on what was at hand.

Still panicked, with my spine beginning to feel like a cold steel rod, I worked more diligently on the quintessential prayer.

"OK," I blurted, sending more steamy puffs of breath into the darkness. "I don't need some outside force now. I need to access the God inside. I need the whole damn battalion of inner troops for this one."

Through the howl of the wind and the crunch of my tires against the snow, I could hear the pounding of my heart, pumping hot red blood through veins tight with fear. Snow swirled in circles like Van Gogh stars, and I crept along through the twilight zone of black and white while new prayers formed in my wrenching gut.

"Road," I whispered, "I am car and tire and I affirm our oneness. We are one whole, moving together, and all is well." I concentrated on becoming the road, the car, and the tires all at once. I was heavy metal moving safely, black round rubber revolving, hugging icy roads that held me—all of us bound in a mysterious embrace. The prayer, which had come not from my head, but from some deep place below, was not about rescue. Not about changing the circumstances. It was simply about accepting the real. Becoming at one with what was around me.

Nothing changed externally. The winds still howled, the snow continued to blow in blinding sheets of white and there was still no red glow ahead signaling the presence of another on the road. As far as I knew, I was the only one in the storm. But being one with the elements made all the difference. Focusing all my attention on the present left no

The longing to tell one's story and the process of telling is symbolically a gesture of longing to recover the past in such a way that one experiences both a sense of reunion and a sense of release.
—bell hooks

Our deepest fear is not that we are inad-equate. Our deepest fear is that we are powerful beyond measure. It is our light, not our darkness, that frightens us. . . . And as we let our light shine, we unconsciously give other people permission to do the same. As we are liberated from our own fear, our presence automatically liberates others.
—Marianne Williamson

energy for fear of the future. If I stayed fully in the present, concentrating only on what was before me, there was no room for anything else, and moment by moment, I began to see that I was safe.

If I could remember this when I start to create—to let only the moment I am in concern me—then I would be free to express with no taint of fear or limitation. But when I come to the table as an artist, I come first with what rests on my surface—fears that I am not worthy or wise enough, doubts that I am capable enough, worries that others will judge my work as worthless or of no use. These are all concerns of the past or the future, taking chunks of my energy which belong to the art, for if I do not bring the whole of me to the work I am creating, the work itself will be only a fragment of the whole that sought in the beginning to be manifest through me. I may, in the presence of fear, create a beautiful poem, but in its absence I might create a masterpiece.

If I come to the work with complete attention, paying no mind to fear or doubt, entering into communion with the Muse and the source of life itself, then I will be able to draw freely and abundantly from wells deeper than my own knowing. I will find, then, that the art seeks me, waiting only for my openness and total present-mindedness.

The stories, songs, and images I want to create live right below my surface, like those seven unicorns in the 3-D picture. In order to access them, I must shift my gaze, refocus, and go beyond the layer of my fears into the realm of what is real, what is present to me now. To create, not looking outward, not with an audience in mind, but with my ears and eyes to the Great Below, becoming myself an audience to the voice of spirit. Listening for words that will rise up from places I know not, for images that will come like strangers in my dreams—colorful, poignant, and full of some purpose that is mine to ponder.

This is the kind of creativity that is energizing. It is free flowing like a mountain stream, governed not by will or intention or sluggish imagination, but bubbling with energy, fast-moving and crystal clear. This is what happens when we take our notebooks, write down a question, ask for an answer, and then write what comes to us as fast as we can. The key is to stop thinking and let the words flow freely, to keep writing every second, even if the words make no sense, until the answer eventually arrives on the page.

Truth flows freely, as does creativity, when we have removed all

---

You simply keep putting down one damn word after the other, as you hear them, as they come to you.
—Anne Lamott

Soul enters life from below, through the cracks, finding an opening into life at the points where smooth functioning breaks down.
—Thomas Moore

I believe that each work of art, whether it is a work of great genius, or something very small, comes to the artist and says, "Here I am. Enflesh me. Give birth to me."
—Madeleine L'Engle

barriers. In the case of truth, we remove illusion; in the case of creativity, we remove fear and doubt. It is our nature to be creative, to find ways of passing on the myths and tragedies and unspeakable beauty in which we find ourselves immersed. While we no longer paint images on the walls of caves as did our ancestors, we do use paints and clay, sounds and movement, music and drama to bear witness to the events that shape our lives. From the smallest of childhood disappointments to the most passionate of love affairs to the most grievous of human injustices—it is all grist for the artist's mill, story after story waiting to be told, reshaped, revisited, redeemed.

Opening ourselves to the gifts of the Muse is an opening to all that has come before as well as to all that has not yet come. It is a bold and adventurous gesture, a sign of our willingness to create, not from our thinking, but from our being. To come at our art like water, not ice, not fixed in a particular shape, but fluid and able to flow with the source. It is to come as a transformer of energy, turning the horror of a tragedy into a poem that can be savored, the sound and sight of war or peace into a song that can be sung forever.

Having done that, having become one with the thing that we shape into art, we are free to let it go, having found what we needed in the lessons it offered.

Art is a collaboration between God and artist and the less the artist does the better.
—Andre Gide

Something sacred, that's it. We ought to be able to say that such and such a painting is as it is, with its capacity for power, because it is "touched by God."
—Pablo Picasso

Dearest Muse,

I believe that the moment
I open myself to your gifts,
I have opened as well to the Source of Life.
I come to you with all my emptiness,
asking that your words flow through me,
your energy fill me,
and the music that you are
sing me awake.

It is my hope that what we create
will be as useful as a hammer,
as honest as a prayer,
far-reaching as a bridge
and urgent as a cry.

My ear is turned to the sound of you
and I bow before you in prayer and praise.

May we together
become one clear light
against the dark,
one breath of fire
against the chill.

Dear Child,

It is only your openness
that is needed for this work,
only your willingness
to go within and
find that beauty
you seek to express.

Remember your oneness
with the Force of Life,
and resist temptation to think
you are separate.

Do not doubt yourself
but let things flow
as a running stream,
not clinging to your words,
judging their worth, but
freeing them to take
the shape they will take.

Be concerned, not with others
as you create, but with your
own truth telling.

I am here to guide
and witness the unfolding
of that truth,
and to remind you that
All is within your reach.

I believe that my work is joyful, useful, and constantly changing,

flowing through me like a river with no beginning and no end.

Your Work Flows Like a River

I went to a photography conference a while ago and attended a workshop for freelancers. It was an opportunity for photographers to hear from and question a panel of picture editors from several major newsstand magazines. They each spoke on the use of pictures in their magazines, what they were looking for, and how they like to be approached by freelancers.

When they opened up for questions from the floor, I was the first to raise my hand in a crowd of about three hundred. I started by saying that I was a writer and photographer and was often in doubt about which editor to query with a story idea—the photo editor or the articles editor. Before I even finished the question, I knew from their body language that I had run amok somewhere. One rolled her eyes, another curled up his lip in a noticeable smirk, a third scanned the audience as if looking for the next question.

One editor took the time to explain the problem with my question. One is either a writer or a photographer, he said with the greatest of authority, and it is not possible to do both well enough to be considered for his publication. The others nodded their heads in agreement, and he went on describing how they look for photographers who specialize in only one subject, be it fashion, cars, documentaries, or dogs. In a nut-shell, they all agreed that an artist can do only one thing well, and anyone who attempts to cross over into other styles or media sacrifices excellence.

Even if only the people in your writing group read your memoirs or stories or novel, even if you only wrote your story so that one day your children will know what life was like when you were a child and you knew the name of every dog in town— still, to have written your version is an honorable thing to have done.
—Anne Lamott

It is the creative potential itself in human beings that is the image of God.
—Mary Daly

In the beginner's mind, there are many possibilities. In the expert's, there are few.
—Shinryu Suzuki

I call intuition cosmic fishing. You feel the nibble, and then you have to hook the fish.
—Buckminster Fuller

I sat down feeling like a country bumpkin in the palace, embarrassed that I had even asked the question. I wondered how Leonardo da Vinci or Michelangelo might have responded to being told that they could do only one thing really well. Not that I place myself in the same category as those two great artists, but I couldn't help thinking what we would be missing out on had either of them been confined to a single medium. Would we have to choose then between *David* and the Sistine Chapel?

My embarrassment at the editors' response soon shifted into disappointment. I had a choice to make. I could pick an area to specialize in, do only that until I achieved mastery while competing with others working in the same domain, or I could follow my inspiration, work on projects that I delighted in, and trust that each piece of work would find its own way into the public eye. That one brief encounter was a pivotal point in my career, where my question changed from What do they want and how can I please them? to What do I have to give and how shall I give it?

I did not want to choose between writing and photography, nor could I. For me, there are days when it is the image I am called to, days when it is the word that beckons, and days when the work clamors for both. I would never sacrifice one form in order to concentrate totally on the other, at least, not now, when I feel so drawn to both of them.

For my work to be joyful and useful, it must come from the inside out, conjured up in response to an inner impulse, not dictated by the market or mainstream media. This does not mean that my work has nothing to do with the outside world. It has everything to do with it— with my perception of it, my fears and dreams for it, and with my belief that our creations have the power to shape and change the world. Not that one piece alone will have a major revolutionary effect on the way things are, but that each piece of writing, each painting, each musical composition, each sculpture that we create and dare to put out there as a form of art has the potential to make a difference in the lives of those who encounter it.

I once happened onto a native Hawaiian festival while riding my Honda on the back roads of Oahu. There were several hula schools performing ancient hula, a dance that does not even remotely resemble the saccharine-sweet ukulele hula performed at all the Kodak spots in

Honolulu. Ancient hula is danced to the beat of drums and the sound of the conch shell. The gestures are broad and powerful, and the women move like barefooted warriors across the wooden stage, their movements swift and sharp as blades cutting the air.

Dancers in Hawaii are often big-bellied women, round and massive in body and spirit, and I was taken in by the beauty and grace of one such dancer whose name was Mapuana. I shot rolls of film of her moving like an earth mother to the pounding drums, her feet adorned with anklets of maile leaves, a lei of pikake on her bountiful breasts, and another garland of maile around her hair. She was the most beautiful dancer I had ever seen.

A few years later, one of these images of Mapuana was published in a series of photographic notecards of women. A while later, I received a letter from a woman about its effect on her. She wrote that she is a big woman and has always hated her body, but that one day she received this card in the mail, and it brought her to tears. "When I saw that picture of Mapuana, I saw myself in her. I saw my beauty and my power, and for the first time in my life, I felt like I could love myself." She keeps it on her altar now as a reminder of all the beauty that big can hold.

Another image in that notecard series is of an old Chinese woman singing opera on a hill in a Beijing park. Her face is as wrinkled as an apple doll, but she is radiant and her eyes twinkle like stars. Someone sent this card to Gloria Steinem, and she wrote about it in her book, *Revolution from Within*. "I have a new role model for this adventurous new country I'm now entering. She is a very old, smiling, wrinkled, rosy, beautiful woman standing in the morning light of a park in Beijing. . . . Now, she smiles at me every morning from my mantel. I love this woman. I like to think that, walking on the path ahead of me, she looks a lot like my future self."

These are just two small examples of how our work can be useful and make a difference in the world, piece by piece. How often it begins simply as a response to something beautiful or tragic or joyful, then takes on a nature of its own, forming itself into a shape that others can experience and find themselves in. In the work we create, there is always the possibility that others will find some meaning they have been seeking, that some new light may be cast on their darkness, or some thrill of recognition may occur as they sense their own feelings in the piece we have created.

Artists in each of the arts seek after and care for nothing but love.
—Marsilio Ficino

One comes to be of just such stuff as that on which the mind is set.
—Upanishads

From Mozart I learned to say important things in a conversational way.
—George Bernard Shaw

*That civilization
perishes in which the
individual thwarts the
revelation of the
universal.*
—*Rabindranath
Tagore*

*Fill your mind with all
peaceful experiences
possible, then make
planned and deliberate
excursions to them in
memory.*
—*Norman Vincent
Peale*

*You are the truth from
foot to brow. Now
what else would you
like to know?*
—*Rumi*

In her book, *Writing Personal Essays*, Sheila Bender writes, "There are feelings and longings we understand and accept in ourselves only when we recognize them in someone else's words, words that never have been ours to speak until we saw them written out of someone else's life." Though we do not set out to touch another's feelings and longings, in the course of finding and revealing our own, words and images rise up that are as universal as they are personal, reaching out beyond the particularities of our lives into the common consciousness, where others can draw on them for strength or sustenance.

I find myself daily in the art of others. I find my sorrow in Segovia's *Recuerdos de la Alhambra.* I find my wonder in Doris Lessing's *Canopus in Argos* series. I find my courage in Wagner's *Pilgrim's Chorus*, my sense of community in Adrienne Rich's poetry and Paul Winter's music, my delight in the artwork of Amy Bartell. I find my fighting spirit in the poems of Sonia Sanchez and Judy Grahn, in the essays of Audre Lorde, and in the music of Sweet Honey in the Rock, Holly Near, and The Flirtations. I find my kinfolk in the paintings of Bonnie Acker, my love for nature in the photographs of Galen Rowell and Thomas D. Mangelsen, and my spirit guides in the sculptures of Tammy Tarbell. I am moved throughout my day by the power of art, inspired by the writers and poets and painters who are creating today as well as by musicians and artists whose works were shaped centuries ago.

When it is my time to create, and I fear that what I have to say will be worth nothing to anyone, I think of these artists who have moved me so deeply. How I look to them for comfort and courage, and how, when I need their words, their music, their images, they are all around me, in every room, on shelves, mantels, altars, walls. I have surrounded myself with their work. And they have, through the years, held me up, sustained me, moved me forward, nourished me, healed me. And this, not because they attempted to fire up the spirit of anyone else, but because they dared let loose their own.

Dear Muse,

So often my work seems a waste of time, so many hours spent in its service when I could be giving my time and attention to people who need it. I sit in my workplace, waiting, wondering, hours passing, little happening, thinking I am not the artist the others are, who have important things to say and shape. Those people whose works flow like a river so sweetly and gently through them to the world. And I, dammed up, feel no flow at all. I feel the sludge weighing me down, the wanting to work but nothing coming, everything held behind the heart.

Please help me break through this frozenness. Help me stop being afraid to let it flow for fear of what may come. Guide my hand in writing freely, my heart in letting go, for when I seize in fear or self-mistrust, that which is waiting is stopped before it has a chance to live. Please help me remember, when I think that others hold the key, that I possess in my own self whatever it is I need to create. I have lived paying attention, and I have noticed what is around me. I have the right to comment, to share what I've seen and heard, been touched and moved by. I believe, in my stronger moments, that what I do can be of use, but when I falter, I need your urging, your sweet reminder that we are all here to share the world we know.

I long for your voice, for that rush of your energy, that free-flowing feeling that comes when I trust my work. Please help me get there. I am so tight and I don't know why. I don't feel afraid, yet the words stay locked inside. I move forward like an old widow with a cane, one faltering step after another. I want to create for the joy of it, for the gift of waking up and knowing that my day will be about newness. I want to let go, to see how things flow, and remember the feeling of the tale telling me. This is the magic I want in my life.

Be with me, please, that I remember the joy and the privilege of creativity, its usefulness, and its constantly changing nature. Thank you for your guiding hand.

Dearest Child,

What you have inside is longing to come out. It is crashing like floodwaters against the gate you hold so tightly closed. When the joy disappears, it is because you have called your work something else, made yourself responsible for something beyond what you feel inside. You know the joy of letting go. You know how smoothly it flows when you give no thought to what comes out, but just let go and let it come. Why is it you keep forgetting and closing down? It serves no purpose. It only keeps you from your work.

I cannot enter into your fear and dispel its power. I can only guide you into your work, remind you what is there to be said, and help you give shape to it. You are an artist because you have chosen to create. Wherever you go, you find beauty that you want to share. That is what your creativity is about, and that is why your struggle is so unnecessary. That which you seek to create already exists. The struggle for you is not to find the words, but to set them free.

When you learn to trust your inner self, this struggle will pass. You will let what is there find its way out, and you will remember again the joyfulness of this labor. You will see that which you have birthed and you will know its value.

I believe that what it is I am called to do

will make itself known when I have made myself ready.

What You Are Called To Do

When the renowned mythologist Joseph Campbell was a young man, he retreated to a cabin in the woods and read for five years. He studied everything he could get his hands on about ancient myths and religions, rituals, art, culture, and anthropology. He was fascinated with the spiritual journey that humankind has been on since the beginning of time and in all the ways that journey has been celebrated and ritualized in every civilization. After those years of reading, he was on fire with what he had learned. He wanted to share his excitement and convey some of the surprising connections that ancient myths have to our modern-day lives, to bring to the present some clues from the past that might guide us in our search for meaningful, joyful lives. But he didn't know how to go about this. He said about that time that he had wished someone would tell him what he *had* to do.

In *Reflections on the Art of Living, A Joseph Campbell Companion*, Campbell is quoted as saying in one of his lectures:

When you come back with a gift and the world, lacking it, doesn't know it needs it, you have three reactions: 1) To hell with them. I'm going back to the woods. 2) What do they want? Create a public career and renounce the jewel. 3) Find some aspect of the domain that can receive the jewel. It requires a great deal of compassion and patience. Look for cracks in the wall and give only to those who are ready to receive.

If you are an artist, you learn how to trap the yearning and put it where you want it, where it goes. That's the secret all true artists come to know.
—**Gail Goodwin**

It is preoccupation with possessions, more than anything else, that prevents us from living freely and nobly.
—**Joseph Campbell**

For those of us who feel that we have some creative gift to offer the world, there is often the temptation to "renounce the jewel" when we find no audience or support for our work. With no ready-made means of supporting ourselves through this work, we often abandon it entirely, thinking if it is not good enough to interest an agent or publisher or gallery, then it is not good enough *period*.

This is the point when many of us give up and choose other professions, leaving no time or energy to devote to our gifts. Eventually we forget we ever had them, forget the inner voice that once called us and the spark of joy we felt in the midst of our creative flurries. What a loss for the rest of us who will never read those words or see those paintings. What a loss for all of us, artist and audience alike.

We live in a culture that does not support the arts, and it *is* difficult to sustain ourselves on artwork alone, but none of us need forfeit our creativity in order to support ourselves financially. I would argue that we need to access our creativity all the more enthusiastically in order to figure out how to support ourselves and our families doing what we love.

As a freelancer, I do occasional articles and photo essays for our daily newspaper on issues that interest me and with which I want to take some time. I pitch the story, get an OK, then start working on it. Once the film is shot and the story written, I deliver them to the newspaper and meet with the editors to review the work.

That trip to the newspaper offices always reminds me of why I remain a freelancer. The photo department is in a state of constant frenzy, planning shoots, inspecting negatives, meeting and assigning deadlines. It's a madhouse. Photographers race around the county shooting whatever they are assigned, like it or not. They get their lists. They take the shots. Rarely is there any time to converse with the subject, as the next shoot is scheduled an hour later and may be thirty miles away.

A few weeks ago, a photographer at the newspaper approached me whining, "It must be nice, shooting only what you want when you want to. I don't have time to work on any of my own stuff, and I have to shoot this crap all day long." He handed me a contact sheet with thirty-six pictures of a new shoe store that opened in the mall.

"Yeah," I said, "but there are trade-offs. You can always count on

Writers in a profit-making economy are an exploitable commodity, whose works are products to be marketed, and are so judged and handled.
—Tillie Olson

Not to dream more boldly may turn out to be, in view of present realities, simply irresponsible.
—George Leonard

We should not have a tin cup out for something as important as the arts in this country, the richest in the world. Creative artists are always begging, but always being used when it's time to show us at our best.
—Leontyne Price

that big paycheck at the end of the week, but I'm never quite sure from one month to the next where my money's going to be coming from. Freelancing is fun but it has its anxieties." He shrugged his shoulders and dashed off, and I walked to the elevator, glad to be leaving the chaos behind.

Risks are part of the deal for anyone trying to live a creative life. There's a book on the market called *Do What You Love and the Money Will Follow*. I believe in that and try my hardest to live in accordance with it, but I have my days of doubt when the book I'd write would be called *Do What You Love and Work Part Time at Something You Like Just To Be Sure*.

The trouble is, every time I start letting my doubt get in the way, it tends to cloud my thinking. I start operating from a deprivation mentality, thinking I had better go out and get a real job with good benefits. Then I start to worry that I'm forty-seven and don't own a house, don't have a pension plan, and don't have a way to get all those things I want—the party barge, the grand piano, those ten acres in the mountains. And I think, The hell with being creative, I should go make money. This lasts until my senses return, and I remember that it's my heart I'm here to follow and that's exactly what I'm doing.

I believe that if we really surrender ourselves to the work we most want to do and do it with all our heart, then in the act of letting go and following our passion we will find, not only great joy and release, but also the means to get by in life. Within that act of faithful abandon lies a reward commensurate with the courage it takes. It is like being on the edge of a cliff and waiting for wings to appear before we jump. We could stand on that edge for the rest of our lives, never knowing the rapture of flight, for the wings do not sprout until we've left the ground.

For the artist, this leap of faith is demanded on many levels. In the process of creation itself, we must abandon our fears in order for the piece to take shape, to get past the voices that say we are not capable or wise or worthy enough. Having done that, having committed ourselves to this creative work, we are then challenged to support ourselves and our families while staying true to our calling.

"It is very difficult to find in the outside world something that matches what the system inside you is yearning for," writes Joseph Campbell. For artists, this is particularly true as we create out of the

We have to go behind what we feel and think, behind what we hope for and aspire to and find what we are. Then we will discover that we are an inevitable fact and must inevitably accomplish certain things, pass through certain experiences, and be ourselves forever.
—Manly P. Hall

Art does not come from thinking, but from responding.
—Corita Kent

A first-rate soup is more creative than a second-rate painting.
—Abraham Maslow

yearning in our own souls and find, more often than not, that there is no home for our work in a marketplace economy.

When the Spirit does not work with the hand, there is no art.
—Leonardo da Vinci

While being published is no measure of our creative abilities, having an audience for our work is often an important part of the creative process. One who journals daily for her own deeper knowing is no less a writer than one who writes murder mysteries for public consumption. If they are both writing, they are both writers, using words to expand possibility in a multitude of directions. But for some artists, to "find that aspect of the domain that can receive the jewel" is a necessary part of the creative process.

My mother has written two books, one an autobiography of her childhood, and the other a biography of my father's life. She does not consider herself a writer. She is just writing the stories down for the grandchildren and great-grandchildren before she forgets them. We self-publish the books and print them twenty or thirty at a time, depending on the family's requests for them. It has never occurred to her to sell them for profit, only to cover the costs of printing and binding. All her work is a labor of love, she says.

As for me, I am writing this book primarily for myself. I know that its real title is *Things I Need to Remember.* I am also invested in getting it out into the world because I believe in the value of sharing our stories. I am fully aware of the contribution that art in all forms has made to my life and, as an artist, I intend for my work to somehow contribute to those who stumble onto it. I trust that those who can use these words will find this book, and those who have no need for it will pass it by, in the same way that I myself feel drawn to certain shelves in a bookstore or to certain exhibits in a gallery, only to find a work that my soul craves.

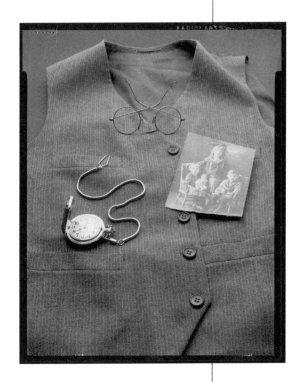

Dear Muse,

I come to you as a student,
eager to learn from
and work with you.
I have tried
in all ways I know
to make myself ready,
to cast out doubts,
to carve out an empty space
in which what is to be born
will be welcomed.
I have tried to clear away
my "knowing" and
leave room for the unexpected.

Whatever it is I am called to do,
I trust will be made known to me,
and I trust as well that you are present
in my life at all times
guiding me to this work.

Dear Child,

When you are ready to answer the call,
you will hear it.
It will come in different forms,
but you will feel the nudge,
that pull at your heart,
that longing to reach down
into the cavernous depths
and find the light
that is yours to shine.

You need not feel alone
on this journey inward,
for I am there with you,
as are many others
whose spirits will guide you
as you move.

Remember that all is One,
that this voice within
is the Voice of All,
the Source of All Sound.
To be in the presence of this,
to add your voice in harmony,
is the greatest bliss.
May you be lost
and found in its rapture.

I believe that the time I spend creating my art

is as precious as the time I spend giving to others.

The Time You Spend Creating Is Precious

aking art is not an act of self-indulgence; it is an act of faith, a movement of the parts toward the whole. To create is to take what we know to the unknown, to mix it up and let it rise. To make art that carries weight, has its own life and power, we must take the seed of experience and plant it, work the soil, wait for germination, summon the Muse, and open the channels for expression.

It is not to say, I have had this moment, this experience, and want to share it, but rather to go into that experience, to study it and find its jewel, to see what it offers that can be of use, and to express that. It is a process that takes time and brings us closer to ourselves as we comb through the past to better understand the present.

When I first started working in the darkroom, I had taken one night-school class in photography where I learned only the basics of exposure, processing, and developing. It was enough to get me hooked, and I was photographing everything in sight. I churned out prints by the dozens, and my family and friends were delighted to get eight-by-ten glossies of everything they were doing.

I had a photographer friend who worked in large format with an old 4x5 camera. I shot circles around her with my Pentax K-1000 while she diligently set up each shot, checked the lighting, arranged the details, moved the tripod, measured the light again, and finally clicked the shutter. She took forever to shoot and would sometimes spend a whole

I have integrated all that was divided within me—a widening of the soul to the dimensions of God.
—Hadewijch of Antwerp

The function of art is to do more than tell it like it is—it's to imagine what is possible.
—bell hooks

day printing one photograph, doing it over and over with more light, less light, changing contrasts, dodging here, burning there. She would come out of her darkroom exhausted, complaining that she did not yet have the perfect print.

I never understood what all the fuss was until I learned more about the art of photography and the power of the medium. While I was shooting for content alone, she was going for all the subtle complexities. She was pulling out the richness of texture, capturing the wide range of tonalities between black and white, closing down her aperture to bring every detail into perfect focus, as the eye would see it in real life.

While my pictures were enlarged snapshots, hers were art, each one deliberately planned and executed. Her images always had a certain depth to them, a reason for the viewer to linger, as they communicated something important about who she was and how she saw the world. Mine were simple reflections of the surface. They said something about the subject, but nothing about myself. They were pictures anyone could have taken. Where she had come as an artist to the craft, I had come as a technician, new to the tools and happy to produce an image that would bring anyone some joy.

Over the years, as I matured in the medium and came to appreciate its potential, my approach changed. I watched my style evolve, saw that who I was had everything to do with what I shot and how I shot it. While stunning landscapes always held a certain appeal, there was nothing as compelling as the intimacy of portraiture. I loved the challenge of those relationships, those opportunities to become so one with my subjects that they trusted me, relaxed with me, as I waited behind my lens for their beauty to shine.

To have this kind of intimacy with people is joyful enough, but then to be able to return to them with an image of themselves in which they feel truly reflected—this is an even greater joy. I have traveled through dozens of cities and have hardly an image of a building or monument, but my files are filled with faces, each of them a memory of a moment of closeness, a chance at communion with a total stranger who let me in long enough to find their spark.

When I am in the darkroom now, I respond as much to myself as to the negatives at hand. Beyond the chemical process, some kind of alchemy occurs as I print, not just for content, but for depth, for

Creativity belongs to the artist in each of us. To create means to relate. The root meaning of the word art is "to fit together" and we all do this every day. Not all of us are painters but we are all artists. Each time we fit things together we are creating— whether it is to make a loaf of bread, a child, a day.
—Corita Kent

Pay attention to what they tell you to forget.
—Muriel Rukeyser

meaning, for revelation of myself and my vision. It becomes a retreat from the world of light and its multiplicity of contrasts to a world without light where there is solitude and singularity of purpose: to connect my parts, to give expression to the voice within that has something to say through this photographic language.

Knowing the power of an image, I try to produce imagery that both reflects my dream and connects with the dreams of the viewer. It is my goal to have others see themselves in my work, to have them feel the commonness with me that I feel with them, to look at one of my photographs and recognize why I took it, what it says, whom it is about. I am trying to drum up feelings of connectedness on a universal scale through the power of a single image, or a group of images combined with words, or images and words and music together. I never know until well into the piece how all the elements will fit together, but the impetus remains the same: to capture an image that speaks of oneness and the common heart.

It took many years before I could think of myself as an artist; it is only since I have identified the yearning behind my work and seen that it touches everything I do, only since I have been able to integrate the work I produce as a photographer or writer with the hopes that rise up out of my own inner darkness, that I may call myself an artist.

This process of integration does not happen easily, nor does it occur in the absence of solitude. On a cultural level, I feel constantly driven from this intimacy with myself. I find little encouragement to arrange my life so there is time to give form to imaginative impulses. Every day I must resist the seduction away from myself and persistently turn to my inner chambers where I experience a truthfulness and wholeness in my life. I know there are thousands of us out there, trying to find the time, the quiet space, the physical energy to respond to the deeper urgings that rise from our center and seek expression. We long to create in our own image, in our own words, to tell our stories in our own styles. But we are one here and one there and one over there. So often we are isolated in our artistry, working other jobs to pay the rent, having children to feed or parents to nurse or hay to be mowed or lovers to be loved, having reason upon reason why we cannot get to our passion, our own work.

I once let my work go for several months and lost the balance in my life. I had begun a new relationship and abandoned my creative work, counting on someone else to fill that spiritual need that can never be met

It's essential that we understand that taking care of the planet will be done as we take care of ourselves. You know that you can't really make much of a difference in things until you change yourself.
—Alice Walker

One is never afraid of the unknown; one is afraid of the known coming to an end.
—Krishnamurti

When the soul wishes to experience something, she throws an image of the experience out before her and enters into her own image.
—Meister Eckhart

by another. I gave all my time and energy to this relationship, never understanding that the source of my truest joy was in my creativity, that it was this work, this play, that made me feel most alive and useful and beautiful. When I neglected it and focused solely on this new love affair, everything fell apart. I became less attractive to my lover, for I was no longer creating work that fired me up and filled me with passion.

It wasn't until the relationship ended that I saw what had happened and began to understand the importance of giving time to my creative work. It took a powerful blow for me to see that I needed to nurture my spirit/self relationship as the primary relationship in my life and the one from which all other intimacies can grow. Without that inner balance, I have no grounding, no real sense of who I am and what I have to offer another.

I was devastated when that relationship ended, for somehow over the course of those months I had lost my center. It was as if I had given my life over to something that was now blown to pieces, and I didn't know how to reassemble it. I had no faith in myself, much less in my ability to create anything of beauty or worth. I knew that I should return to my work, but I was terrified. I was afraid to go into the dark again, for it was no longer familiar. I needed to regain the part of me I had lost, but had no idea where to look. I doubted everything: my vision, my value, the worth of anything I had ever done. It wasn't just that I had to begin again. I had to get past the voices that said there was nothing there to begin with.

Weeks later at an antiques show, I spotted a pair of tiny black patent-leather shoes that looked just like the ones I wore when I was four years old. I bought the shoes and put them in my camera bag when I got home. That weekend, I took them on a photo shoot, placing them in locations where I might have worn them as a child. I photographed the shoes at a playground, under a swing, walking up the slide steps, at the beach, looking out at the sea, in front of a door that was closed and locked.

At each location, as I carefully positioned the black patent leathers with the pink insoles, I felt all the feelings that went with those little shoes—the fears of a four-year-old who feels abandoned, alone, locked out; fears that were as alive then as they had been thirty years ago. I photographed my way through those feelings, crying and mumbling as

Art to me was a state, it didn't need to be an accomplishment. By any of the standards of production, achievement, performance, I was not an artist. But I always thought of myself as one.
—Margaret Anderson

To express the emotions of life is to live. To express the life of emotions is to make art.
—Jane Heap

Art is made real by those who make it real and important to themselves.
—Harold Taylor

if someone were there to hear, for it felt that way, like I was not alone. At the end of the day, I packed the little shoes back into my camera bag, drove home, and entered the darkroom for the first time in months.

I talked to myself the whole time I processed the film—about what it means to be an artist, how it's not about the final piece but all those steps that lead to it: how the magic of creating occurs in the process, not before or after, but every single minute we are doing it; how all the while we are creating, there is only life going on. There is no room for fear, no space for doubt. All our energy is going into the creation. I talked my way through that first critical passage and stayed there for hours, getting reacquainted with the darkness and its healing subtleties.

Those photographs never became part of an exhibition. They have never been published. But they are always near me, always reminding me to give time to my work, to stay balanced, to let it heal me.

One glance at a picture of those little shoes, and I remember that I owe to my creative spirit all the time and tenderness I would give my dearest beloved. One is as precious as the other.

I carried those little black shoes in my bag for a long time. The last shot of them was on a peak in the Himalayas at fourteen thousand feet. They had gone as far as they needed to go, so I gave them away to a little girl I met on the trail. They fit her bare feet perfectly, and she ran off beaming with joy to show her mother.

The farthest horizons of our hopes and fears are cobbled by our poems, carved from the rock experiences of our daily lives.
—Audre Lorde

Dear Muse,

I feel called to this work,
but the call of others who need me
so often takes me from it.
I need your guidance.
I need you to help me remember
that what I create also contributes,
that it is not a waste of time.

I have been trained forever
to respond to others,
to put my own needs on hold
until those of the rest are fully met.
I have been trained to be the keeper
of my sisters and brothers,
never told by a soul
that art had a place
as near to God as service.

I have been shaped by the art
I've found in my life,
needed the books that have come my way,
clung to the music, the paintings, and poems
where I found parts of myself
lost so long ago.

Please help me remember
that what I make
can be of use
and that the time I spend creating my work
is as precious as the time I spend
giving to others.

Dear Child,

There is no reason for you to be torn
about time, for you know
when you are called to this work,
you have a right to whatever time it takes
to create.
Do not be overly concerned about the needs of others.
Those who rely on you will not go hungry or cold.
You have too much love for this to happen.
They may not have all they want from you,
but you will give them what they need.
And they will learn from you
the blessing of creativity,
finding, through your example,
the path to their own magic.
Give yourself freely to this work,
you are here to cocreate the world,
to add your vision, to make visible
what is not yet seen, to manifest that
which is within you.
This is the gift you have for the world.
It is precious and worthy of your time.

I believe that what truly matters in the making of art is

not what the final piece looks like or sounds like,

not what it is worth or not worth, but what newness gets added

to the universe in the process of the piece itself becoming.

What Matters Is the Newness

The artist Wassily Kandinsky writes in *Concerning the Spiritual in Art* that "the artist must search deeply into his own soul, develop and tend it, so that his art has something to clothe, and does not remain a glove without a hand. . . . The artist must have something to say, for mastery over form is not his goal but rather the adapting of form to its inner meaning."

What we have to say with our art runs the same gamut of possibilities as what we have to say in our conversations. Our art may reflect the idle chatter of a cocktail party or the revealing insights of an intimate conversation. We may create art for art's sake or we may create with a deeper sense of purpose, to see what evolves when one's artistic impulse is taken to a level below the surface. Either way, we are creating, but one may take us places the other does not.

To give our art something to clothe, we must know from the outset what its purpose is. Not to know what the final piece will look like, but to know at the beginning what it means to convey—to have tasted it already in our throats, heard its roar, felt the pounding beat of it.

Muriel Rukeyser, in *The Life of Poetry*, writes that "a work of art is one through which the consciousness of the artist is able to give its emotions to anyone who is prepared to receive them." As we deliberate

The small selves and the Great Self are finally one, for as She bodies forth in us, all the beings respond in the bodying forth of their diverse creative work that makes the world.
—Rosemary Radford Ruether

The object of art is to give life a shape.
—Jean Anouilh

over the choice of colors in a painting or chords in a musical composition, we reckon with the emotions that each evokes, attempting to make the outer work as true to the inner feeling as possible. There is a reason an artist chooses cerulean blue over the more vibrant ultramarine, or the passionate vermilion over the more stately alizarin crimson. There is a reason why Dixieland jazz is written in major keys and *Moonlight Sonata* is in minor. There are moods, nuances, subtleties to convey that underline whatever might be called the content of the work. These fine distinctions are what all creative people deal with constantly in the development of their work.

In her book, *What Is Found There*, poet Adrienne Rich gives voice to several artists addressing the questions of form, content, and purpose in their work. Sculptor and printmaker Elizabeth Catlett writes, "I learned that my sculpture and my prints had to be based on the needs of people. These needs determine what I do. Some artists say they express themselves: they just reflect their environment. We all live in a given moment in history and what we do reflects what level we are on at that moment. You must, as an artist, consciously determine where your own level is."

Rich conjectures that by "level," Catlett means two things: first, the sociohistorical roots of our creativity—what traditions we come from, what social privileges we enjoy, and how our social standing affects our art-making process—and second, our level of responsiveness or responsibility to the world around us. To Rich, it means that the artist is "free to become artistically more complex, serious, and integrated when most aware of the great questions of her, of his, own time." She includes comments by poet and painter Michele Gibbs who addresses the question of Catlett's levels:

> Choosing to be an artist (i.e., a distiller and creator rather than an imitator, copyist, critic, or technician) is, itself, a level. Then arise questions of: 1) What are you calling attention to? 2) What energy/action does your creation feed? 3) What reach will your creations (voice/images) have and where are you directing their force? 4) What counts for connection?

To come to our work from this framework, with these questions in mind, is a compelling challenge. It means that we take total responsibility for our creations, knowing full well the force and energy they carry with them. For me first to ask myself, What do I want to call attention to? sets the stage for the right-mindedness with which I hope to create. If I ponder in advance what action I want to feed or where I want to direct the force of my work, I am embracing the idea that my artwork matters in the world, is not frivolous, has an impact.

By determining for myself what counts for connection, I am able to say, *This audience is sufficient, this forum is appropriate*; and to create my own unique arenas for sharing my work. Rich notes that the issue of connection here "implies the centrality of communality in the artistic process," where the authenticity of her vision is verified by the "parallel/complementary creation of others." What I put out into the world, once you receive it, has an impact on what you in turn put back into the world.

We may or may not remember this as we begin our work, but artists who create with this in mind have a great deal to contribute to the well-being of the human family. No matter what the specific substance of our work, if we approach it with an intention of usefulness beyond self-expression, then we breathe into it an air of universality, a chance that it will matter to more than ourselves that the piece was shaped, the spirit released.

Our task as artists is not to respond to the clamor and demand of contemporary public passions, producing earth tones one year, mauves the next. It is not to see what is selling and add to the heap, but to feel for what is missing and bring something to the emptiness. Our challenge is not to look across the landscape of human experience, but to look into it with our deepest compassion and vision, to burrow down into it until we feel the longings of the lost and hear the hungry heartfelt questions of our young.

Art that arises from this place does more than mirror the signs of our times. It is more than an echo of what is already sounding. Art that blends inner knowing with outer experience is fertile and carries with it prophetic strength: the ability to be not merely a child of the present but a mother of the future. It can carry us forward, teach us, move us to action, change the direction of thought and feeling. This art, whose roots grow deep in the common ground, is sustaining art, renewing art, art that carries the promise of a new day dawning.

The creative process, so far as we are able to follow it at all, consists in the unconscious activation of an archetypal image, and in elaborating and shaping this image into the finished work. By giving it shape, the artist translates it into the language of the present, and so makes it possible for us to find our way back to the deepest springs of life.
—*C. G. Jung*

Painting is a faith, and it imposes the duty to disregard public opinion.
—*Vincent van Gogh*

Dear Muse,

I am often troubled
at the beginning
about what the ending will be.
I am troubled
about what will become of a piece,
who will want it, if it will
ever be seen or heard.
I do not want to keep creating
that which sees no light of day,
that which finds no ear to hear,
nor heart to hold.
Of what use are these works
if others do not share them?
What is their worth if they go nowhere?
Is it that I am not good enough?
Is it that the world is not ready
or wanting this that I make
from the love of my heart?
Shall I go out to serve in another way?
Give my time to those who cannot read?
Take food and woolly clothing
to those who are cold and hungry in the night?
Is that the truer calling?
It is my aim to be of service.
Where shall I go with the gifts of my soul?

Dear Child,

When you set out in your work,
set out to find something new
and concern yourself
only with this discovery.
As you create, give thought
to that which is before you
and only that.
You cannot know
the reach of your work,
nor its weight or worth,
so there shall be no arrogance about it,
nor any doubt.
What matters is not what you make
but that you take the tools in your hand,
listen to the voice that calls,
and give shape to whatever is awaiting form.

Look inside and see what moves you,
what makes you cry
for sadness or joy,
and respond to that,
letting your response flow
without judgment or worry.

In the giving of yourself to this work,
give bravely and with honest passion
and what will come will be a gift,
not only for yourself
but for those in your midst
who have hungered for this work.

I believe that I am not alone in my attempts to create

and that once I begin the work, settle into the strangeness,

the words will take shape, the form find life, and the spirit take flight.

You Are Not Alone

It does not occur to me that I am alone when I create, for the process itself always seems to get its jump start from some place other than my own will. Some impulse is already underway before it meets with my intention and gets propelled into what might be called creative work. This inner urging, the push that compels me to add what I have seen or felt or thought to the cosmic mix, is what calls me to the task and what makes me believe there is some other hand in this besides my own.

Coming to the work with a sense of another near me, an image of the Muse hovering at my shoulder, does not mean it all flows freely and smoothly into place. The start is always slow and laborious, for rarely in the beginning is there much to work with. Maybe one phrase, one chord of a song, one bare memory that clamors for attention. When I begin, I do not feel the comfort of a companion or the creative assistance of a fellow collaborator. I feel alone, a fragile ego, with nothing but a strange sense that there is something waiting to be said, some formless thing awaiting my hands to give it shape. And I am no sculptor of words or clay.

Trying to get at it, I hammer out a few phrases at the keyboard, hoping for the sound and feel of grace in motion, but there is only the timid, tinny ring of my own shallowness. I wait for what wants to emerge, but more often than not, nothing comes. I hate this waiting. It makes me thirsty, so I get up and go to the refrigerator. I pour some juice and notice the dishes need doing. I fill up the sink with sudsy water and wash

I am one of those who never knows the direction of my journey until I have almost arrived.
—Anna Louise Strong

Writing is easy: all you do is sit staring at the blank sheet of paper until the drops of blood form on your forehead.
—Gene Fowler

away, still waiting. I remember a friend saying once, "If you wait for inspiration, you're not a writer, you're a waiter."

When the dishes are done, I return to the desk, write some more words and embarrass myself with ineptness. I turn on the music, light a candle, and wait some more. Still nothing. I think of the clothes that need washing. I go to the basement to sort whites from darks and put in a batch of towels. I think I should get a real job and stop fooling myself. Why is it I feel a call but can't hear the words?

I go back for another shot at it, but the desk seems cluttered and in need of straightening. I sort through all the papers and decide to pay my bills and create a newsletter. I leave Microsoft Word for Quark Xpress and start to design a masthead. This does not help. I go to my file of quotes, looking for the wisdom of others to keep me on track. I read through the words of my mentors, scanning for clues on how to break through this maddening silence.

Consuelo Kanaga writes that if she could make one true, quiet photograph, she would prefer it to having a lot of answers. At this point, I feel the same about one true sentence. Doris Lessing says that we must have a vision to build toward and that vision must spring from the nature of the world we live in. In her experience, she feels she is not having a thought, but that there is a thought around. I like this concept and wonder if maybe I'm tuning into a thought that was not meant for me. Maybe I took in a creative nudge that was meant for someone down the street.

A Course in Miracles says that from far off in the universe, yet not beyond myself, the witnesses to my teaching have gathered to help me learn. I wonder where they've gathered and why I wasn't invited.

Next it's Deena Metzger who writes that to be an artist is to be loyal to a vision when it presents itself, no matter how disruptive or disturbing it may be. I'd like to know if her visions come in full-length cinema or pop in and out like mine do, like ten-second PSAs. I swear I'd be loyal to a vision if I could just hold onto one long enough to get a sense of what it is. Denise Levertov doesn't help much by saying that one of the obligations of the writer is to say or sing all that he or she can, to deal with as much of the world as becomes possible to him or her in language. Language is just the thing I'm having trouble with. Where do I find this voice in which to deal with the world?

There are very few human beings who receive the truth, complete and staggering, by instant illumination. Most of them acquire it fragment by fragment on a small scale, by successive developments, cellularly, like a laborious mosaic.
—Anaïs Nin

Art, it seems to me, should simplify. That, indeed, is very near the whole of the higher artistic process; finding what conventions of form and what detail one can do without and yet preserve the spirit of the whole—so that all that one has suppressed and cut away is there to the reader's consciousness as much as if it were in type on the page.
—Willa Cather

Finally I come across Nancy Mairs, whose spin on the writer's voice question gives me hope. In response to a student's question, "How did you find your voice?" she writes:

> *As though "you" were a coherent entity already existing at some original point, who had only to open her mouth and agitate her vocal chords—or, to be precise, pick up her fingers and diddle the keys—to call the world she had in mind into being. Not just a writer, an Author. But I've examined this process over and over in myself, and the direction of this authorial plot simply doesn't ring true. In the beginning, remember, was the Word. Not me. And the question, properly phrased, should probably be asked of my voice: "How did you find (devise, invent, contrive) your Nancy?"*

I'm comforted by this, thinking it may be true, not just some figment of my fanciful imagination, that there really is some voice trying to find me, calling for me to speak of that which I don't yet know. And then a quote from bell hooks pops out from the page:

> *Often I felt as though I was in a trance at my typewriter, that the shape of a particular memory was decided not by my conscious mind but by all that is dark and deep within me, unconscious but present. It was the act of making it present, bringing it out in the open, so to speak, that was liberating.*

So now I'm thinking I should go back to the keyboard, try to stay out of the way, and let my own unconscious voice have its say. To see what flows when I just let go and stop trying to get it right. I tell myself I am not out to change the world, but simply to add a piece of myself to it. That I can write for the joy of it, to see what happens when my mind meets up with the voice within, when it is not just me calling upon the Muse, but the Muse calling upon me as well.

I think of the writings that have shaped my life and of all the writers who have written their way through whatever fear gripped them. I think of those who continued to write in the face of self-doubt or repeated rejection from publishers. Of those who wrote because writing called

No artist is pleased. . . . There is only a queer divine dissatisfaction, a blessed unrest that keeps us marching and makes us more alive than any other human beings.
—*Martha Graham*

We are not to fear the strangeness we feel. The future enters into us long before it happens.
—*Rainer Maria Rilke*

One has to have a bit of neurosis to go on being an artist. A balanced human seldom produces art. It's that imbalance which impels us.
—*Beverly Pepper*

them and would not let them go. Those who wrote to release themselves from ghosts of the past and whose words enabled hundreds of us in hundreds of cities to let loose our own ghosts.

I imagine these writers in this same struggle, pacing their wooden floors, torn with doubt, hurling crumpled papers against dimly lit walls; yet here on my shelves, printed and bound, are the words they put down in the face of this battle. Words I have cherished, needed, returned to over and over again. They never knew they were writing for me, but they must have known they were writing for someone because they didn't give up. They wrote their way right through that fear and I think, If they did it, so can I. I can work with this one thought, stay with it, play with it, until it begins to take its own shape. I know it will take shape because it always goes like that. It starts out with a tiny fragment that I hold in my mind, but then I get seized up, convinced that I can't do well by it. I stutter and stammer, my words flowing not like the river they want to be but dammed up by an inner critic who stops every one in midstream. I am like the poet to whom Friedrich Schiller wrote, "Your problem is that you bring in the critical factor before the lyric factor has had a chance to express itself."

I read Natalie Goldberg and Anne Lamott and all the others who say that this will happen but write anyway; just keep writing until you get to the other side of it. I want to, but something inside me has more power than good sense, and days go by when I might as well have been playing in mud for all the clarity I've achieved. I've read that the closer we get to something that's difficult to write, the more fervently we should push through, focus on what's hardest to say, and just blurt it out.

So here I am trying to blurt out this paradox of how I believe I'm not alone in my attempts to create, while I have felt basically abandoned by my Muse throughout this whole chapter. And I suppose she would say the same, that I am the one who has abandoned the work—leaving the post regularly to do the laundry, wash the kitchen floor, call my mother, scrub the bathroom, rub my cat's head, go for groceries—instead of sitting still and settling into it. She would probably also say that if I gave her half the chance I give my critic, we would probably get where we are going a lot sooner.

The thing about this belief is that, even when it doesn't feel like

Looking back, I imagine I was always writing. Twaddle it was, too. But better far write twaddle or anything, than nothing at all.
—Katherine Mansfield

One must avoid ambition in order to write, otherwise something else is the goal: some kind of power beyond the power of language.
—Cynthia Ozick

If I take the wings of the morning and settle on the farthest sea, even there your hand shall lead me.
—Psalm 139:9–10

someone's really there, words somehow keep coming out of somewhere. If I just dig in my heels and go at it, even if the only thing I can write about is the difficulty of writing, then at least there is some movement, and the words have a chance to flow where they want. This is the best I can do as a writer, or as a creator of anything in any medium—just open the gates and let loose whatever wants to move.

Dear Muse,

Where is it you've gone
that the fire seems doused
and the air holds no spark
of thought or dream?

Where is it you've gone
that my memories turned to dust
and no word makes its way
but the lonely howl of loss?

Are you there in the trembling?
Is your hand reaching out?
Can you feel this fear
or hear this doubt,
are you close enough
to touch this hollow?

Will you come back
if I go on without you,
if I jump from the ledge
and dare what follows?

Will you come back
from what place you've gone to,
come back bringing roses
and fire and tea?

My Child,

Do not linger at the gate
awaiting my return
for it is only your feelings
that have me be gone.

In truth I am always
at your side
though you feel loss or hunger
for some raging fire.

Remember that all you need
you have inside,
that wisdom you long for
you already own.

Do not imagine
you are nothing without me,
but that you're everything with me,
as I am with you.

When you leave the ledge
and jumping, face the great unknown,
you will know that I have never left,
that my wings were ever 'round you
till you bravely grew your own.

I believe that as the Muse gives to me,

so does she deserve from me:

faith, mindfulness, and enduring commitment.

As the Muse Gives, So Does She Deserve

When I was first opening up to the concept of the Muse, first really feeling her force in my life, I was writing to her in my notebook one morning, asking questions about issues and decisions with which I was struggling. I was trying to keep my own thoughts out of the way and let her answers flow through my pen when suddenly a whole flurry of words filled the page. I was not thinking then, not trying to compose something, but only recording what I felt coming through as it passed, and these are the words that ran like a river across the page:

> *Now is the time to be mindful of light*
> *to keep the flame going, to give up the fight*
> *for life is a pleasure, it's not meant for pain*
> *let go of the struggle and dance once again*
>
> *For you all have an angel who sits at your side,*
> *who waits for your calling, who hears every cry.*
> *She's there at your service, there as your guide*
> *so call her, she's waiting with arms opened wide.*
>
> *The God that you're seeking needs not to be sought*
> *you're already one like the sea and the salt*

The work of art which I do not make, none other will ever make it.
—Simone Weil

Great art is the expression of a solution of the conflict between the demands of the world without and that within.
—Edith Hamilton

*the Source is within you, the force is at hand
it's been in your soul since your life began.*

*So rejoice, my child, in the gifts that you have
the light of the world is the torch in your hand
and when you get beyond your fear and your pain,
you'll see God in the being who goes by your name.*

I was quite flabbergasted that it all happened so fast, and that it came out in rhyming poetry, which I don't ordinarily appreciate. I went for my guitar to see if it might be a song and sure enough, the chords were right there, and everything fit perfectly into place. There was no struggle about it, no straining for the right fit. It simply worked.

It was that experience that led to my perception of the Muse as a real presence in my life, a kind of partner or collaborator in the creative process. I began to relate to her as one would relate to any new friend. I made time for our relationship, wrote to her in my journal, asked her questions, and even felt that the responses I scribbled into my notebook might truly be coming from her, or from that place in me that was not accessible through the usual channels of consciousness.

When I asked what her name was, the answer seemed to come back "Rebecca," so I started calling her that. I sang her little songs as I drove around, thanked her for her presence in my life, and rearranged my work schedule so I would have more time for quiet and a better chance of hearing her. Over the next months, in collaboration with my newfound friend, I wrote a few more songs and recorded an album of original music, produced two video documentaries, edited a women artists' datebook, started an original screenplay, and finished graduate school. It was a time of high energy and extraordinary productivity.

That summer, at the International Women's Writing Guild Conference in Skidmore, I taught a workshop called "Marry Your Muse," hoping to assist other women in moving closer to their own sources of inspiration. There were fifteen of us, and when we began, some of the women were not even sure what a Muse was. I shared what mine was to me, and a few other women in the class talked about the Muses in their lives. Some of them had names for their Muses, some had complete images of what they looked like, what they wore and the color of their

---

The seeker, however, must seek—and this is the core of his difficulty. He cannot know what he is looking for until he finds it.
—William Segal

All striving must be directed against littleness, for it requires vigilance to protect your magnitude in this world.
—A Course in Miracles

You only need claim the events of your life to make yourself yours. When you truly possess all you have been and done, which may take some time, you are fierce with reality.
—Florida Scott-Maxwell

hair. Some just had a feeling of her. Others only a longing for her presence.

We spent the week using music, art, and writing to fire up our imaginations and open up our relationships with our resident Muses. We started with prayers, candles, songs, invited them in, thanked them for coming, wrote to them, asked them our questions, pondered their answers. For five days we played with our Muses, learned their names, danced with them, and created with them.

On the last day, we had a commitment ceremony. As we stood in a circle around a candle, a bowl of water, a few acorns, and a feather, each woman made a vow to her Muse, symbolizing her commitment to her creative work and process.

"I vow to set aside one hour for you each day, that I might hear your words and write with your fire."

" I vow to keep believing in you, even when I do not feel you there."

"I vow to honor you by finishing the novel I have been working on for five years."

"I vow to tear up all my rejection letters and to stop doubting that I have something important to say."

"I vow that I will have more fun in my life, that I will stop being afraid of what others think, and that I will turn to you in the light as well as in the dark."

"I vow that I need you, that I honor your presence, and that I will come to my work believing I am not alone."

"I vow that I will not let my husband and children come in the way of my relationship with you, and that I will share you with them in whatever way I can."

"I vow that I will stop spending time reading how-to articles and spend it on writing what I have to say."

"I vow to live with my full attention and to write the truth of my own experience, however difficult that may be."

"I vow my joy to you, and my gratitude for having found you. I will never let you go."

"I vow to call on you daily, to keep my ears tuned to your quiet voice, and to dance with you at least once a week."

"I vow the end of my fear, the end of my depression, the end of my isolation. I vow, with your help, to find the support I have been needing."

Everyone has been made for some particular work and the desire for that work has been put in every heart.
—Rumi

Why is it when we talk to God we are said to be praying and when God talks to us we're said to be schizophrenic?
—Lily Tomlin

The goal of life is rapture. Art is the way we experience it. Art is the transforming experience.
—Joseph Campbell

I am not a writer except when I write.
—Juan Carlos Onetti

"I vow to be as present to you as you are to me."

"I vow that when I hit a wall in my writing, I will not stop, but break right through it with your strength as my own."

"I vow not to forget this week, to keep a picture of this group on my altar so I will never again think I am alone."

There is an energy in the creative process that belongs in the league of those energies which can uplift, unify, and harmonize all of us. . . . If the job is done well, the work of art gives us an experience of wholeness called ecstasy, a moment of rising above our feelings of separateness, competition, divisiveness to a state of exalted delight in which normal understanding is felt to be surpassed.

—Corita Kent

It was one week after that workshop that I wrote the Artist's Creed, half feeling it was my gift to the Muse, half feeling it was her gift to me. Either way, it didn't matter. I was just happy to have something I could send these women, to remind them of their commitments and to address all those things they said over and over again got in the way of doing their work: no time, no place to work, not enough quiet, not enough confidence, no trust in the value of their work, no certainty about where it was going or if it was useful.

Someone once said about the Artist's Creed that it seemed more selfish than not, more about me than about God—the one who really should be praised for creativity. I was embarrassed and didn't know how to respond, but I felt bad that she missed the point—that it is totally about God, the God within us, the God, the Muse-Who-Is-Us, who is the fullness within our emptiness, the aching within our desire. Not who we reach for, but the act of our reaching. And that all of our creative work is not the result of some external force that arrives to inspire and assist us, but of some miraculous opening within ourselves that allows our own vision and beauty to shine forth.

The faith that is called for in the creative process is not a faith in something beyond us, but a faith in our ability to let loose the light within, a faith strong enough to overcome the myth that the Great Power is beyond us. Strong enough to keep us at our work when the voices outside and within would have us believe it is worth nothing. This faith, this kind of mindfulness, is contrary to public opinion, not popular, even blasphemous to some.

In the midst of recording "Rebecca's Song," which is the song that begins this chapter, the pianist who was accompanying me stopped the taping to tell me he thought what I was singing was heresy. He was a Catholic so immersed in the concept of an external God that he could not allow the possibility of an immanent presence, a God within.

This kind of thinking has so damaged us as a culture that to dare internalize a power as great as God, to dare say that we create out of our own nothingness, our own emptiness which is the temple of the Source—this to some seems unimaginable, profane. And it is in this environment that we learn to devise other points of reference.

So I speak of the Muse, I call on her, I light a candle to signify my openness to her, I leave spaces between my lines for her, I thank her, and all the while I know deep inside that this Muse is not beyond me, not outside, nor inside, but of me. This *we* of which I speak is not this *I* and this *she* who write. This *we* is the writing, the word enfleshing itself, the act of creation.

And the work we do—creators everywhere who dare or dare not call themselves artists—these paintings, this music, these sculptures, these words that unravel and wrap and lift and bring tears and redemption, these things are the world being created, yet anew, every day.

PRAYER TO THE MUSE

I seek you in all I do
that I don't miss red
on the winging blackbird,
or the green leaf sprouting
after winter's chill.

I seek you
that I notice mauve in the light
of the dying day
and gold in the hour
of the one being born.

I seek you in all I do
that I hear the whoosh of the hawk
as he dives for his prey,
the cry of the child
whose mouth I might feed.

I seek you
that I touch the shoulders
of those craving touch
and sing to the ones
whose ears cry for sound.

I seek you
like night seeks dawn,
like fire seeks air,
and birds the sky,
and fish the sea.

Already there, I am
the pilgrim seeking the journey.

Already found, I am
the one in search of the finding.

PART TWO

Staying on the Path

At the end of each chapter in this section is a series of suggested reflections and exercises designed to stimulate creative thought and activity. As art tends to stimulate art, these exercises often involve the use of other art forms. You are invited to write, listen to music, and watch films that deal with some of the issues addressed in this book.

For the writing exercises, I suggest that you purchase a notebook specifically for them. Your words and thoughts on these matters are important enough to warrant their own notebook, and for the journey you'll be on, you'll want to take notes. Find something that feels good on your lap, looks attractive, and is small enough to fit in your backpack or purse if you're one of those who writes on the move. And splurge on a pen you really love—one that fits your hand like it was made for you and writes with the color ink you most love to see. Set it up for yourself so that everything about this writing is beautiful and fun and worthy of all you bring to it.

As for the music, although I recommend specific tapes or CDs, don't feel you must rush out and buy every one. These are pieces that have served me on the way, stirred my emotions, and moved me closer to my own truths. What works for me may work for you, and so might other music that you already possess and love.

The point is to use music as a tool, to let it wash over us and into us and set free the feelings that often get lodged in our deeper places. To be able to access these feelings is an important step in the creation of our art and ourselves, as it is often from our emotions that our truest voices emerge.

You usually think that your feelings about a given event are primarily reactions to the event itself. It seldom occurs to you that the feelings themselves might be primary and that the particular event was somehow a response to your emotions, rather than the other way around. The all-important matter of your focus is largely responsible for your interpretation of any event. . . . When you fulfill your own abilities, when you express your personal idealism through acting it out to the best of your ability in your daily life, then you are changing the world for the better.

Jane Roberts, *The Individual and the Nature of Mass Events* (from the Seth material)

Letting the Heart Sound the Beat

Over the years, I have received phone calls from women preparing for global journeys, ready to make some incredible difference in a foreign land, to leave the mark of their compassion and commitment. They have read my book, *Making Peace: One Woman's Journey Around the World*, and are looking for tips on how to do it. Can I meet them for lunch, give them advice over the phone, send them a letter full of addresses and helpful hints? Immediately I see myself in them—younger, driven to give, to shine their light and balance the darkness, eager for advice about where to go, whom to meet, how to make their way in another culture. I wonder at times where any of us finds the courage to

There is a change coming in the lives of girls and women, and it is up to us to make it happen.
—Alice Munro

make such a journey; then I remember this Jane Roberts quote from the Seth material, and the answer begins to unfold.

Ironically enough, it was not simply the urge to go somewhere, but the urge to leave something as well that precipitated my own trek across four continents. I was in the throes of a dying relationship and didn't have a clue how to resolve things. Travel always seemed like a good idea when I was fumbling around with fear and intimacy, but I had no plans, no sense of direction.

Then one day, someone left a copy of *The Hundredth Monkey* on my workbench in a picture-framing gallery. I opened it up on my lunch hour and read a story about a research project that was being carried out by American scientists on monkeys who lived on a group of islands off the coast of Japan. It was never clear why they were doing this research, but the story goes like this:

The researchers put out sweet potatoes for the monkeys and watched their behavior. What they noticed was that the monkeys gobbled up the potatoes, dirt and all, and thoroughly enjoyed this new treat. One day, an eighteen-month-old girl monkey named Imo took her potato down to a stream and washed it off. She found it much more pleasant to eat the potato without all the dirt and sand attached, so she taught this behavior to her mother and her young friends, who in turn taught it to their mothers. Within a couple weeks, many of the monkeys were washing their sweet potatoes before eating them.

Then a few weeks later an amazing thing happened. One monkey, hypothetically referred to as the "hundredth monkey," picked up her sweet potato and washed it off, and at that moment an evolutionary breakthrough occurred in this tribe of monkeys. From that moment on, all the monkeys washed their potatoes before eating them. Even more amazing, the scientists noticed that within a couple of weeks, this behavior had spread to all the monkeys on all the islands.

In his analysis, author Ken Keyes, Jr. writes:

When a certain critical number achieves an awareness, this new awareness may be communicated from mind to mind. . . . When only a limited number of people know of a new way, it may remain the consciousness property of these people. But there is a point at which if only one more person tunes into a new aware-

The real voyage of discovery consists not in seeking new landscapes but in having new eyes.
—Marcel Proust

People do things, one of which might be writing, to help themselves and other people ask questions about who they are, who they might be, what kind of world they want to create, to remind ourselves that we do create the world.
—Barbara Christian

Stop thinking and talking about it and there is nothing you will not be able to know.
—Zen proverb

ness, a field is strengthened so that this awareness reaches almost everyone. Individuals can communicate private information to each other even though located in different places. The strength of this extrasensory communication can be amplified to a powerfully effective level when the consciousness of the "hundredth person" is added.

When I finished reading this story I shivered with delight, thinking that if it was true for monkeys, it might be true for humans as well, so I decided to experiment with being the "hundredth person." I would travel and meet with groups of people, communicating on whatever level I could something about making peace during a frightening era of nuclear madness. That afternoon, I went to the bank and started a savings account for a trip around the world—a journey that would change, more than anything else, my own awareness of who I was.

My fear of intimacy, that urge to go, that book at that time—all factored equally in making it happen. People have often said how courageous it was to venture out alone into foreign lands, but the truth is, that for me, the courage would have been in staying home. To go was the easy thing.

In this situation, as Seth suggests, feelings were the primary thing; the particular event, the journey, was a response to those emotions. All my life I'd been religiously conditioned to act from my mind, not my feelings. From an early age, I was taught to do what was charitable, not what I wanted; although, luckily for me, the two often coincided. But because I had a constant companion in my head reminding me that the noble thing was to do what was generous or kind, not what I felt like doing, I never learned how to trust my feelings.

I could not allow myself the freedom of just leaving—leaving the relationship, leaving for an adventure, leaving behind doubts and questions for which I had no answers. At that time, it would have felt cowardly and self-serving. So I was rescued, in a sense, by *The Hundredth Monkey*. On one level, it offered a very real and new source of hope to a young activist looking for ways to patch together pieces of a fractured world. On another level, it provided an acceptable and somewhat honorable reason for leaving. I was now planning a trip that was, symbolically at least, for others as well as for myself.

Writers are the moral purifiers of the culture. We may not be pure ourselves but we must tell the truth, which is a purifying act.
—*Rita Mae Brown*

Power is the ability to take one's place in whatever discourse is essential to action and the right to have one's part matter.
—*Carolyn Heilbrun*

Your first job is to get your own story straight.
—*Natalie Goldberg*

The quest is not merely to discover the treasure for oneself, but to share it with others, "to enter the city with bliss-bestowing hands."
—*William Segal*

On that trip I would learn my lessons, see myself against a foreign backdrop where my flaws shone like jewels on a velvet cloth. I would discover that the real work was to make peace in my own heart and that the only way to do this was to free my feelings—to entertain them, nourish them, come to know and trust them. As I learned to do this, I saw how others were freed in the process.

In Nagasaki, I was invited to present a slideshow and speak to a group of atomic bomb survivors about the peace movement in the United States. Before my presentation, we watched a film that had been produced using recently released military footage of Nagasaki the day after the bombing. Gasps and quiet sobs punctuated the darkness as people in the room saw themselves, forty years earlier, stumbling through burning rubble, calling out for families they would never see again. I had never felt so much pain in a group. When the lights came up and I was introduced, I looked out at their faces, scarred and disfigured, and started to cry. I wanted to say, "Here, look at these pictures. See what we are doing, millions of us, organizing, marching in the streets, so it doesn't happen again." But I just stood there looking at them, tears running down my crumpled face, as I said, "I'm so sorry. I'm so sorry."

And they cried too, wiping their faces, nodding, and gesturing with their hands for me to go on. And when they saw the slides, saw for the first time what people around the world were doing for peace, they cried again. What we shared there, with all our feelings breaking loose, felt like a redemption, a release that allowed the pain we'd been holding to pass through and beyond us, at least for a time. In that moment of awful and awesome transparency, our oneness had a chance to emerge. As we dropped our armor and shed our tears, a wall that had kept us separate came down.

Time and again, from country to country, group to group, it happened that way. The more I dared to speak from my heart and expose my emotions, the more others did the same. It was a remarkable discovery. While I had once spent great effort in denying my feelings, I was beginning to see they were a gift to be shared. A good place to start from in a crowd of strangers.

I wasn't, after all, traveling as a teacher or a wise one with answers. I was there as an artist with pictures and music and questions to share,

A perception, sudden as blinking, that subject and object are one, will lead to a deeply mysterious wordless understanding; and by this understanding you will awaken to the truth.
—*Huang Po*

If we had a keen vision and feeling of all ordinary life, it would be like hearing the grass grow and the squirrel's heartbeat and we should die of that roar which lies on the other side of silence.
—*George Eliot*

Life is either a daring adventure or it is nothing.
—*Helen Keller*

mining for the solutions we held in our hearts. As I told the story of the hundredth monkey and how I believed in our power to change things, I revealed myself constantly, sharing fears and dreams that others might too. In the process of listening and letting go, I learned that feelings often lead to answers, are often home to the wisdom we look elsewhere to find. Though I started with the dream of changing the world, it was I who was altered as I grew to love what I had learned to deny.

Now when these young travelers call seeking advice, I smile at my end of the line and applaud them for acting. I imagine there is something deeper going on than their urge to help, some feeling that is calling them away from or toward the great unknown. They are ready for an epic adventure, and whatever happens, they will profit from it and be forever changed.

It hardly matters what we call our mission, whether it's ourselves or others we set out to help, or if it's fear and doubt that lead us to action. What matters is that, whatever our fear, we make our way to the edge of the cliff and, looking beyond, dare to jump. For that is the action that calls forth wings. They do not sprout till we have left the ground.

This is true for all of us whether we journey or not. Perhaps for some the edge of the cliff is a poem that is stirring or a song waiting to be given life. Perhaps for others it is an honest conversation or a display of feelings that have long been suppressed. Great things happen when we give them life. Great openings occur for the Muse to enter when we free our hearts and let the graces flow.

If you are going to act on the basis of what you know, you cannot just hold onto your knowledge. You have to translate it into a movement.
—Joseph Campbell

Meditations and Actions

1. Listen to *Journey to Antarctica* on the CD or tape *Polar Shift— A Benefit for Antarctica* (Private Music). Close your eyes and imagine your own journey through your daily life. Reflect on these questions: Where are you heading? Why are you going there? What do you need for the journey? What do you have to share? How does it feel to be going there? Are you alone? With others? What new things do you want to be learning? What will you be teaching? If it helps, write your answers in your notebook as the music is playing.

2. List five major events in your life and see if you can name the feelings that precipitated them. Did you value those feelings then? How do you perceive those feelings now?

3. Have a conversation with a person of the opposite sex about feelings. Ask how that person views his or her feelings, whether they are frightened by them, whether they deny them or act on them. Share your own thoughts and feelings about your feelings and see what common ground you have in the matter.

4. How do you express your personal idealism? Think of the last time you were involved in a project that reflected your commitment to something. Did this make any difference in your life? What are you committed to now and what are you doing to express that commitment?

5. Rent the video *Now Voyager* (Warners 1942) and watch it with a friend. Look for the transformation in Bette Davis as she claims her life and lets her feelings surface. When the movie is over, discuss it with your video buddy and see what new insights might evolve.

6. Listen to Paul Winter's *Missa Gaia /Earth Mass* (Living Music Records). For the first five to ten minutes, close your eyes and just let yourself *be* with the music. Then, in your notebook, write down the Seth quote from the beginning of this chapter. Without stopping to think or edit, write down your feelings about this until you have filled two pages. What did you learn about your thoughts?

Mom's Advice

"When someone asks you to do a favor," my mom advised from her chair at the sewing machine, a place where she regularly handed out morsels of wisdom as if they were M&Ms meant to sweeten our days, "never ask what it is first. Always give a cheerful 'Sure, if I can,' and try to figure out how to do it."

"Yeah, but," I'd start, with two of the most common words in my adolescent vocabulary, "what if you're busy doing something that's really important?"

"Now think about it," she'd say, her hands poking at the wad of material under the sewing machine foot. "What could you be doing that would be more important than doing a favor for someone?"

That kind of thinking always left me blank. "Yeah, I guess you're right," I'd say, shrugging my shoulders and slumping off, feeling like some kind of selfish sinner for thinking of myself first.

My mom dispatched a lot of philosophy from the Singer sewing machine that doubled as a podium, and the underlying theme of most of it was, "Remember: the other person is more important than you are." Now, I'm sure this is what she learned from her dad, whose job it was to lead fourteen children down the straight and narrow with as many memorable bits of wisdom as possible. In fact, my mom would often preface her remarks with the phrase: "My father used to say . . ." and end with ". . . and you know how wise grandpa was," pretty much eliminating any room for discussion on the subject.

The words of our mothers do not fade over time, but grow like acorns into sturdy oaks, their roots ever reaching into the soil of our lives. I ended up being a fairly popular teenager, meeting the needs of everyone else with the enthusiasm of a zealot while my own projects waited. My mother's philosophy was consistent with everything I was learning from the nuns at St. Anthony's, so I trusted it was good and practiced it religiously. I believed that others were more important than

Women in particular must not allow our integrities to be formed by the spurious lesson we have been taught that we should be more for others than for ourselves.
—Carter Heyward

Without stories, a woman is lost when she comes to make the important decisions of her life. . . . Without stories, she cannot understand herself. She is closed in silence. . . . Women often live out inauthentic stories provided by a culture they did not create. The princess married and lived happily ever after.
—Carol Christ

me, that it was better to give than to receive, and that when I did something good for others it was like doing it for God, and how could I not?

It's not that I wasn't conflicted at times, or that I didn't get tired of giving and occasionally serve myself first. But deep down inside, I really believed that denying myself was the right choice, the more Christlike way to be. And God knows that was my goal, a mission I pursued with vigorous commitment for the next twenty years, until I learned a valuable lesson in a Japanese monastery.

I was staying in a community in the Japanese Alps founded by a Roman Catholic priest turned Buddhist monk. Every night, eight of us shared a meal, then sat in a circle and discussed issues that had some bearing on our spiritual lives. Being a spiritual adventurer, I was delighted to delve into Buddhist philosophy, eager to see what it asked for and offered, but I experienced some conflict when I tried to mesh the principles of an inner-centered Buddhism with my outer-directed Christianity. I was not trying to choose between the two, but rather to see how they were linked and to fortify myself by incorporating the wisdom and strengths of both views.

Though I had long abandoned affiliation with any religious institution, I found that immersing myself in an unfamiliar religion exposed the underpinnings of my own religious values. Until I was in a Buddhist context, I could not see the claim that Christianity had on my life—a claim that was not so much intellectual as cellular, propelling my movement if not my conscious thoughts. While the Buddhists around me were calmly seeking to be and to accept, I was relentlessly seeking to do and to change. As they sat in quiet embrace of the world's reality, I floundered about noisily, trying to alter it. My call was a version of the Biblical mandate to "go and teach all nations," while theirs was a call to stillness and silence. But what was the right way? Which path should I travel? Was this trip around the world, this peace pilgrimage I had started only weeks before, a futile gesture, a waste of time that would be better spent elsewhere? This was a conflict I could not resolve.

One day, while doing chores with Father Oshida, I asked if he could help me with my latest dilemma. "Of course," he said, tending to the wheat sheaves he was spreading out to dry. "What trouble are you having?"

The very nature of creation is not a performing glory on the outside; it's a painful, difficult search within.
—Louise Nevelson

It is not the world we live in that counts; it is the way we live in the world that is important.
—Manly P. Hall

Poetry allows one to speak with the voice of power that isn't granted to one by the culture.
—Linda McCarriston

All language is a longing for home.
—Rumi

All my life, I told him, when given a choice, I had tried to choose what I thought Jesus would choose. I had tried to be selfless, as I was taught, and to do what I could to make things better for those around me, which had led to a life of social activism. Now, I confessed, I didn't know what to do. On the one hand, I believed that one person could make a difference in the world, as had Jesus and Gandhi and Dr. Martin Luther King, Jr. But being in a Buddhist environment had led me to question whether it was better to be mindful and accepting of things as they are or to get out there and try to make some changes.

"What I'm trying to say," I blurted, "is that I don't know what to do or how to be anymore. I don't even know if I should continue this trip." Father Oshida continued to lay out the grain, nodding his head and carefully arranging each sheaf so that it faced the sun. "We are not called to be like Christ, but to *be* Christ. And we do this by being most truly ourselves—not by trying to be one way or another, but by being fully aware of who we are and responding to all things from that awareness."

"How do I know if I'm doing it well?"

"You know because you are at peace with yourself, having responded to the voice of your own heart."

"But doesn't God want us to think of others first and take care of them before ourselves? Aren't we supposed to be doing what we can to make the world a better place?"

"The point is not to convert the world, but to convert our souls to God, to see everything as the Incarnation. It is not to interpret things literally with our minds, but to go deeper and experience wisdom. Sometimes when we do that, it takes us away from the world into our own quiet places where we are not always available to others. It is from that silence that we learn what is next for us, where our path is leading, and how we can be of service."

I spent the next day in silence, reconsidering values that had shaped the contours of my life. I wrestled with the question of being and doing, searching not for what was right but for what seemed the better fit. I reflected about time, pondering when to give and when to take it, what I owed to myself, what I owed to others. I questioned the sacrosanct notion that the needs of others were more important than my own, and with the care of a gardener committed to life, I started pruning the outgrowth from my mother's words. One by one, I pared away beliefs that no longer

You don't have to think about doing the right thing. If you're for the right thing, then you do it without thinking.
—*Maya Angelou*

God is not attained by a process of addition to anything in the soul, but by a process of subtraction.
—*Meister Eckhart*

Don't seek for truth. Just drop your illusions.
—*Zen saying*

Live your life as you see fit. That's not selfish. Selfish is to demand that others live their lives as you see fit.
—*Anthony DeMello*

felt appropriate, ideas from the past that had been handed down as truth by those who never thought to question.

Adding East to my West, I burrowed down into a faith that had taught me to reach out, discovering that depth was as crucial as height, and silence as vital as speech. As I began to understand the distinction between being like Christ and *being* Christ, I felt a certain relief, no longer needing to labor over what someone else would do in a particular situation, but trusting my own instincts as I honored myself along with the others. My task was to transform the inner voice into outer action, to go to the desert when necessary, to attend to others when that was the call. It was not a matter of putting others before myself out of some selfless striving, but of remaining true to the work to which I am called.

I stayed one more day at the monastery, then left, confident that my place was on the road. The Buddhists had offered a new framework for making choices, an invitation to sanctify my own life, to value its worth. During those few days of meditation, prayer, and silence, I learned a lesson I had never learned from my mother or the nuns at school. I learned that our choices must rise up from within our hearts, not as gestures of self-surrender, but as expressions of our grandest selves, honoring the sacredness of who we are.

And while I know this to be true and cling to this belief with a powerful urgency, I struggle still to choose myself when another calls. Struggle to say no, to value my work, to lay time at my own doorstep when there is any left to give. Old voices die hard. Though it is the words of the Buddhist I strive to remember, it's my mom at the sewing machine I always hear.

Many of us have difficulty putting ourselves first when it comes to prioritizing time, especially when it involves time for creative projects that are not in themselves profitable. For some reason, it is harder to justify this time, particularly when we have children, parents, lovers, or friends in need who would be well served by our precious attention. Here's how a typical conversation might go between two voices in one head:

"You need to be making money, so don't go spending your time on projects that lead to nothing."

"I may not be getting paid to do this, but who knows, if I do it well enough, someone might want it."

If we go down into ourselves, we find that we possess exactly what we desire.
—*Simone Weil*

I don't know what your destiny will be, but one thing I know: the only ones among you who will be truly happy are those who have sought and found how to serve.
—*Albert Schweitzer*

"Are you kidding? Who would want something you make? Do you honestly think you have something worthwhile to say?"

"Yes. Well, some days I do."

"Well, not today. Have you listened to your answering machine? You have a dozen calls. People all over town need you to do things for them, and that's what you should be doing. Your kids need to be picked up. Your mother is lonely again. Your husband is golfing. You need groceries and the laundry is piling up."

"Look, I just want one hour of time alone. Is that too much to ask?"

"Given the needs of everyone around you, I'd say it was pretty selfish, wouldn't you?"

"One hour out of twenty-four? You think that's selfish?"

"Why don't you take it after everyone's in bed? Then it won't matter."

"Don't you think I'd like to do something creative when I myself have some energy? I'm exhausted by the time everyone else is in bed!"

"There you go, thinking of yourself again."

"All right, you win. Where's that grocery list?"

Meditations and Actions

1. In your notebook, write down the conversation that occurs between you and the voice that tries to keep you from your creative work. (You will probably find that this takes no time at all, since that voice is very near the surface and quite outspoken.) Once you have finished recording the conversation, underline all the negative things that have been said about your creative work. Make a list of these phrases and, next to each one, write down what you really believe to be true (e.g., Sing professionally? You can't even carry a tune! / My voice is healing and beautiful and people love to hear me sing). When you have all your true beliefs listed, write them on a small card and place them on your altar or workspace where you can see them and be reminded of your own gifts.

2. Put on some music, light a candle, and in your notebook draw a

It is not because things are difficult that we do not dare, it is because we do not dare that things are difficult.
—*Seneca*

If you are fully alive, alert, and responsive to the challenge of every moment, then you are living a spiritual life.
—*David Steindl-Rast*

picture that represents you as a child. Then, surrounding that picture, draw pictures of the people who gave you advice. In cartoon bubbles, write out their advice.

Notice what pieces of advice you still follow today. Is it good advice? Does it contribute to your well-being? Would you want your child to live according to this advice?

3. Consider the quote by Meister Eckhart, "God is not attained by a process of addition to anything in the soul, but by a process of subtraction." If, in order to attain a more peaceful state of being, you were able to eliminate five distractions from your life, what five things would you get rid of? Write these down in your notebook. If they were eliminated, what would you do with the time they had previously consumed? What prevents you from using your time in the way you truly desire?

4. Take one week in your calendar and make appointments for all the things you'd like to be doing in an average week. Include time for reading or exercise or writing as if these were the priorities in your life, as important as business meetings or doctor's appointments. Follow this schedule for one week, honoring your meetings with yourself. If someone calls and asks you to do something during one of your scheduled events, feel free to say, "Sorry, I have a meeting then." Notice if you feel any differently about yourself at the end of the week. If it works well for you, keep doing it.

5. Make a lunch date with a friend or two to talk about the subject of taking time for yourselves. Share the difficulties that come up around this issue and brainstorm ways to support each other in making time for your own personal projects.

Music Suggestions

Anonymous Four, *An English Ladymass* (Harmonia Mundi)

Meditation, *Classical Relaxation*, vol. 10 (Delta Music)

Andres Segovia, *The Romantic Guitar*, Segovia Collection, vol. 9 (MCA Records)

Carlos Nakai, *Emergence* (Canyon Records)

Earth Songs, *Narada Collection* (Narada)

Chip Davis, *Sunday Morning Coffee—Day Parts* (American Gramaphone Records)

Kitaro, *Toward the West* (Geffen Records)

Pablo Casals, *Encore* (SONY Music Entertainment)

Vangelis, *Opera Sauvage* (Poly Gram Records)

Loreena McKennit, *The Visit* (Warner Brothers)

Giving the Artist Within Half a Chance

I have never been trained in art criticism. Nor would I want to be. I don't even like the concept. I think it has led to too many people saying things like, "I'm not creative. I don't have any artistic talent. I can't draw. I could never be an artist." Can you imagine someone saying to a young cave dweller with tools in hand, "No, that's not how you draw a buffalo. It's supposed to look like this"? Or to an aboriginal child learning the ancient chants, "No, no, that's not how it's supposed to sound. You must sing it this way." The most beautiful art comes from our deepest, rawest selves; it rises from within like the hoot of an owl or the song of a whale.

We have created in our culture an institution called "art" for the sake of commerce and economy. Let us not confuse this with the art of our lives. Let us not be limited in our self-expression by those whose work it is to judge or profit from the creations of a choice few. That is only one aspect of a multifaceted jewel.

Each of us is born to create. Every living being has some gift to express that will benefit the whole, and it is for each of us to discern what gifts we bring to the table. This indeed is the hardest work—not the actual doing or being, but knowing what it is that we are called to be and do.

We often get confused by money, by how we make our living, thinking that who we are is what we do. I may be a pipe fitter, a school bus driver, an accountant, a nurse's aide, or a retail buyer, but beyond this, there is something else, something deeper. Beyond this role for which I get paid and by which I make my way in the world, there is an urge waiting for expression, a story waiting to be told.

As embarrassed as I am to admit it, I once heard these words coming out of my mouth in a conversation with a friend: "I wish someone would tell me I had to write a novel. I wish they'd assign it to me, like a task,

Once you have chosen what you cannot complete alone, you are no longer alone.
—A Course in Miracles

Keep away from people who try to belittle your ambitions. Small people always do that, but the really great make you feel that you, too, can become great.
—Mark Twain

Fiction and poetry written by women may come to be viewed as sacred texts of a new spiritual consciousness.
—Naomi Goldenberg

Clean your ears. Don't listen for something you've heard before.
—Rumi

Your poems will happen when no one is there.
—May Sarton

What another would have done as well as you, do not do it. What another would have said as well as you, do not say it. What another would have written as well, do not write it. Be faithful to that which exists nowhere but in your-self—and thus make yourself indispensable.
—André Gide

A critic is a legless man who teaches running.
—Channing Pollock

like some kind of voluntary service that would be as good for the community as giving blood. I wish I was needed for something like that."

If someone had said that to me I would have been all over them. "What do you mean you're waiting for an assignment? You think you might have a novel in there and you haven't started yet? Novels *are* as important as blood in this world—haven't they shaped your life, taken you to new worlds, inspired action, uprooted your anger, informed your choices, brought you to tears, shed light on your dark? And what do you mean 'good for the community'? Don't you get it that for you to do exactly what keeps you happy is one of the best ways you can be good for the community? That's the biggest thing we *do* need from you. So when are you going to start?"

Now, if I have a hard time heeding artistic urges, I have to know there are a lot of us out there in the same kind of trouble. The same excuses control us and keep us silent. *I'm not good enough. I don't have time. It's not important work. I'm not creative enough. Others do it better.* As if the work is only about product, only about the final thing we end up with in our hands. And we already know how it won't stand up.

Every time I walk down a bookstore aisle and see books on creativity, I'm ready to give up. *It's already been done. She probably said it better. He's probably an expert, and I'm only someone who calls herself an artist.* How soon I forget that what I make from my experience is original art. It can never be duplicated, for no one in the world will experience life in the same way I do. How I write about it, see it, photograph it, sing it, dance it, sculpt it—as universal as the creation may be, it is unique because it came out of an experience that no one else has ever had—mine.

Sometimes I think that if every person in the universe truly manifested their creative powers, if each of us took seriously our role as creator and created as if the world depended upon us, then maybe that is all it would take to bring order to the chaos. Maybe that would be enough to end all wars, for it is impossible to be engaged in the act of creation while simultaneously destroying the beauty before us.

But because we live in a profit-centered culture, there are few voices calling for the works of the people. Mass media is interested in the gaudy details of the rich and famous. Newspapers and magazines peddle horror, death, and conflict as if they served us. Beauty does not sell, nor does depth, nor tributes to kind and courageous acts, though we need these now more than ever before.

In these times, we would do well to create with no regard for profit or fame, to create from our own urgency to communicate something of beauty, to add something of value to a world that is going under for lack of it. It is time now to see what you can contribute and to discern where it is needed. Do not sit on your dreams as I did, waiting for someone to say, "We need this from you." The people are unaware of their deepest needs right now; it runs amok like a satellite out of orbit, oblivious of the error. But what is inside you now, what you pray about, what you cry over in the fearful moments, what so touches your tender heart—these things are the materials of your creations.

Dig into your deep down. See what is there to be expressed and what medium it wants for expression. Forget the art teachers, the choir directors, the critics, the editors, the publishers—all the people who have led you over the years to believe you are not good enough. All the artists of the world who create for the sake of creating call on you to do your part. It's time now to join the circle, find your voice, use your gifts. You have waited long enough. We need you.

Meditations and Actions

1. If you were stranded on a desert island with all the food you needed and in no danger, how would you self-express? What would you want to communicate? Spend a few minutes writing about this in your notebook. Play music. Light the candle.

2. Rent the video *Portrait of the Artist: Georgia O'Keeffe* (Educational Broadcasting Corporation) from your local library. See if there are any similarities between what she was up against and what you feel up against in your creative work. Look for documentaries on other artists and notice how each of them overcame his or her barriers.

If Galileo had said in verse that the world moved, the Inquisition might have left him alone.
—*Thomas Hardy*

How can I know what I think unless I see what I write?
—*Erica Jong*

Look within. Within is the fountain of good, and it will ever bubble up, if thou wilt ever dig.
—*Marcus Aurelius*

Let a guide direct you who only has at interest your getting lost.
—*Myra Shapiro*

3. Imagine that you are one of twelve survivors of a global holocaust and that it is your collective task to reconstruct a new culture. What particular gifts would you bring to the task and what role would you like to play in the process of rebuilding?

4. If it was your job to create a piece of work that would communicate something about life in the 1990s on Planet Earth to visitors from another planet, what might your piece look like? Would it be a song, a poem, a dance, a novel? Why not join with five other artists and create a group exhibition on this subject (or any subject) for your local gallery? Or with a few other writers do a reading at your local bookstore?

5. If you were to design an ideal studio in which to create your art, what would the studio look like? Where would it be? How often would you go there? Draw a picture of your ideal work space in your notebook. Be sure to include all the essentials. What is it that keeps you from creating such a space for yourself?

6. What are the minimal requirements for you to do your work? Do you have them? Do you use them? If you had a chance to lead a workshop on creativity, what five things would you be sure to cover? How do these things affect your work?

7. Go to your sacred space, light a candle and put on some music. In your notebook, begin a conversation with your Muse in which you ask your big questions. Listen to her responses and write them down as they come.

Music Suggestions

African Voices, Songs of Life (Narada)

Handel, *Water Music* (Seraphim Records)

A Different Mozart—A Contemporary Collection (Poly Gram Records)

Hidden Beauty—A Narada Collection (Narada)

Sanctuary—20 Years of Windham Hill (Windham Hill)

Paul Winter, *A Concert for the Earth* (Earth Music Productions)

Vangelis, *Antarctica* (Poly Gram Records)

Kitaro, *Silk Road* (Geffen Records)

Karafan, *Adagio* (Deutsche Grammophon)

Start Anyway

Over and over again, it happens in the same way. I feel the tiniest tug of a creative urge. I wake up and feel the call. There is something to write, something to photograph, a poem, a song—something wanting life nags at my heart, and I sit there. Waiting. Waiting for it to pull itself together and let me know how to get it down. I wait for inspiration. I wait for the piece to get assembled in my mind and days go by when nothing happens. But the knowing is there.

I feel the push of the formless thing within, this inchoate force that begs for life, calling on me to give it form while I, not knowing, wonder how. This thing calls for my power, for the shape I can give it with the curve of my hand or the stroke of my brush. It calls to be born through me, in me, with me, a wisp of spirit seeking flesh.

In these early stages of a work being born, no memory of creative delight eases the fear. No image of joy over past accomplishments rises up to shroud the barrenness ahead. Each time we begin, we begin anew, alone, afraid. Teilhard de Chardin, a Jesuit scientist who brought to his work the passion of an artist and faith of a mystic, wrote of the creative process in *The Divine Milieu*:

> *Work is always accompanied by the painful pangs of birth. To create, or organize material, energy or truth, or beauty, brings with it an inner torment which prevents those who face its hazards from sinking into the quiet, closed in life wherein grows the vice of self regard and attachment. An honest worker . . . must learn continually to jettison the form which his labor or art first took and go in search of new forms. Over and over he must go beyond himself, tear himself away from himself, leaving behind him his most cherished beginnings.*

Giving shape to the voice within often involves many beginnings.

We don't see things as they are, we see them as we are.
—*Anaïs Nin*

There will be narratives of female lives only when women no longer live their lives isolated in the houses and the stories of men.
—*Carolyn Heilbrun*

The writer's job is to see the see the bleak unspeakable stuff, and to turn the unspeakable into words—not just into any words but if we can, into rhythm and blues.
—*Anne Lamott*

What might start as a story may crave to be a poem. What might have felt like a sonata may end up a cantata. Once we step past our fear and enter in, art takes on a life of its own. It will not pull itself together while we wait on the sidelines. It will not self-express while we wait for inspiration, but only begin to take on shape as we move in to meet it. Waiting only keeps the magic from happening.

Igor Stravinsky, in his *Memoirs and Commentaries*, wrote about his work: "My knowledge is activity. I discover it as I work, and know it while I am discovering it, but only in a very different way before and after. I do not try to 'think' in advance. I only start to work and hope to leap a little in my spirit." This is the scary part, starting to work with little to go on but that tug at the bones—that one haunting phrase, that one recurring chord, that one distinct memory. It is in our nature to want to see where we're going and how we will get there. Few start a journey without a map. But in the creative experience, there are no maps. There is only the act of leaping in, answering the call and going where it takes us.

The actual process of creating, once one has fully entered into it, can be an exhilarating experience. When I dare to let the words find their own rhythm and give vent to emotions as they emerge in their rawness, a certain joy tumbles in on the heels of such abandon. Letting out the first draft can be as healing as a primal scream if we do, in fact, let it out, allow its passion, make room for its cry as it finds its voice. We may whirl like dervishes, spun by the tale, lost in its pace and pulsing beat as the truth from below rises up.

Nell Blaine describes it aptly in Eleanor Munro's *Originals: American Women Artists*: "*Organic* is a word I'll stick by. It means the work is an extension of your blood and body; it has the rhythm of nature. This is something artists don't talk about much and it's not even well understood: the fact that there exists a state of feeling and that when you reach it, when you hit it, you can't go wrong."

This is the feeling all artists yearn for, the grace we pray be showered upon us. For it is not something to be conjured through will or desire. It comes, I believe, in response to our trust. Trust in the voice beneath our own, trust in our ability to get out of the way, trust in the stories that knock at our doors. It comes when we let go of our ego and damning critics and simply let flow our rivers of truth.

When we allow our passions, our stories, and our words the freedom they deserve, we allow ourselves the possibility of authentic creativity. Not when we edit as we go, foraging through Roget's for the perfect word, while the flow is stopped, the heart put on hold. Not when we worry what the final piece will look like, who will like it, if it will sell. Not when we look out to see who is listening, but when we look within to see who is speaking. When we have it right, when we are fully attentive, not to our fears but to our guiding forces, then we feel the joy, sense the wonder that creation can be.

Ask any child. When children are painting or building castles of sand, there is nothing but fun going on. They are humming, licking their lips as they ponder each move, making big decisions about brown or sienna or just how wide to make their moat. They don't look at each other's work and compare. They don't wonder if Mommy will like it. Or worry that trees are not really purple. They are in love with the moment, thrilled at the chance to be making it up. There is no ego here. No child in the corner crying about not being good enough. They know what we as adults have long forgotten: that they all have a right to create what they want, and whatever they make is true and good.

Creativity is work of the heart, unrelated to the economy of our ordinary lives. It is not about ego, not about money or success or failure. It is a calling from the spirit, a chance at one of life's powerful experiences, to make something whole from the pieces of our lives.

In the creative process, we are called to cocreate with the thing that wants birthing. We must listen, open ourselves, summon courage, commit ourselves to the task, and begin. And this is the hardest part: in the face of nothing, we must begin. Not waiting for the sentence to be fully formed before writing the first word. Not waiting for the completed image to manifest in our minds before approaching the canvas.

We must begin and let the spirit of the piece interweave with our own. This is the mystery of art. This is its rapture. It is the flesh in a dance with spirit, the ultimate embrace out of which comes a work as pure as our intent, as inspired as our openness. There is more power here than anywhere else. There is mystery here, magic, life-altering possibilities, and it is common to feel unequal to the task.

But what we forget is that we are not called upon to create alone. There is the piece itself beckoning us, the *David* that lived within the

If people knew how hard I worked to get my mastery, it wouldn't seem so wonderful at all.
—*Michelangelo*

How can I know what I think till I see what I say?
—*E. M. Forster*

If you do not tell the truth about yourself, you cannot tell it about other people.
—*Virginia Woolf*

I suppose I have written novels to find out what I thought about something, and poems to find out what I felt about something.
—*May Sarton*

marble before Michelangelo's touch. Michelangelo was called to the stone not knowing what he would find, but he started anyway. And that is our task. To start anyway.

I shall say what I feel and talk about myself unto the last page, and I shall make no apologies.
—Elizabeth Smart

Meditations and Actions

1. You are asked to be on a panel with the theme: "Can art change the world?" Create an outline for your presentation.

2. Go to your local crafts or art supply store and buy a package of modeling clay. While listening to your favorite classical composition or one of the pieces recommended at the end of this section, create something from the clay that says something about who you are. It could be an image of yourself, of something you love, of an abstract form that feels good in your hands. Feel free with the clay and see what happens. Place whatever you create on your altar or in your sacred space.

3. Invite some friends over for an evening or afternoon of creating. Provide paper, paints, colors, clay, pastels. Put on some music and see what happens. Ask people to draw a picture that represents heaven, sculpt an image of something they love, paint something they are thankful for, draw and color a map of where they've been and where they are going, or anything you or they want to make up. The point is to come together for a creative exercise and to share your expressions and what it felt like to create them.

4. You are about to be given $25,000 to produce a work of art in any medium you choose. You have all the time and all the tools you will need, even a crew if necessary. It is not meant to serve any purpose other than to be a work of original art. What will this project look like?

5. Get your notebook. Make a list of some of the artistic work you have created over the years. Include poems, stories, novels,

songs, paintings, sculptures, etc. Think about the process of creating each of them and of how you might describe that. Ask these questions about the pieces: Who did I do them for? Was I paid, and did that make the work harder or easier? Which piece was most fun to work on? Which most reflects who I am as a human being? Which feels least like me? Which am I most proud of? Least proud of? What words do I use to describe my artistic process? Do they sound more like work or fun?

6. A young artist writes to you for advice. She wants to be a writer, but people keep saying she can't earn a good living that way. She looks to you for some guidance. Write her a letter expressing your feelings on the subject. Don't forget your music and candle.

7. Identify a living artist whose work has affected your life. Make arrangements to visit, call, or write to that artist and let her/him know the impact of their work on you.

Music Suggestions

Enya, *Watermark* (Reprise Records)
Suzanne Ciani, *Neverland* (Private Music)
Benedictine Monks of Santo Domingo, *Ave Maria* (Milan Records)
Dan Gibson's *Solitudes—Journey with the Whales* (Solitudes Ltd.)
Kitaro, *Ten Years* (Geffen Records)
Spencer Brewer, *Romantic Interludes* (Narada Lotus)
Rachmaninoff, *Vespers Evening Star* (Philips)
Jean Pierre Rampal, *Italian Flute Concertos* (SONY Classical)
Gustav Holst, *The Planets* (Deutsche Grammophon)
Yo Yo Ma and Emanuel Ax, *Cello Sonatas* (BMG Classics)

We see in the symbolism of sacred art the transmission of ideas directly into the emotions of man, into the "heart" that can speak in active voice to the intellect that chooses and is able to attend, to listen to it. Yet perhaps more essential even than art or verbal formulations is the establishment of conditions of living that reflect truth, the truth about ourselves—conditions that make listening possible.

Sacred Tradition and Present Need, ed. by
Jacob Needleman and Dennis Lewis

Leaving the Chaos Behind

In the matter of the arts, before we can speak, we must first hear. Before we can hear, we must first be silent. And before we can be silent, we must first leave the chaos.

It may be possible to create a symphony while sitting in the Calcutta train station, but it is a harder task there to leave the chaos behind. Better, if we are committed to creating, to prepare a space where the energy goes into creation rather than overcoming the clutter of sights and sounds.

One day in the midst of a creative meltdown, I decided to transform our guest bedroom into a sacred space, having come to the delusion that the barrier to my success was the lack of such a space. If Virginia Woolf couldn't manage without a room of her own, how could I be expected to?

I went at it with a vengeance, tearing down the bed, hauling up rugs, removing artwork, heaving dressers into other rooms, stripping the space of any signs of its former life. Once I was down to the bare floor and four walls, I felt a great freedom rise up. Not only did I have the whole room

I learned to think of God as a woman and by that simple experience I discovered I could begin to think of God.
—Jane O'Reilly

to play with, I had the privilege of designing the ultimate space for creative thinking.

Wanting to make the room as Zenlike as possible, I went for a minimalist feel. No rugs, one lamp, one wooden rocking chair, and a table that would serve as an altar on which I'd place some candles, small rocks and feathers from favorite places, an incense burner, a few photographs, a goddess statue, and a clay container for the scraps of paper on which I scribbled my prayers and intentions. I had a cassette deck for music and a big box of candles that I would burn lavishly.

I loved going into this space, loved how the aroma of frankincense lingered, loved the stillness, the lack of distraction, the feel of holy, and the sound of empty. I didn't work here, but I prepared for work, invited the spirit, opened my arms. I'd sit and rock and listen and watch, the candle flickering, the smoke swirling upward, the wall between two worlds growing ever thinner. I went there often, retreating from the day's noise, advancing toward an inner solace. Driving home from work, I looked forward to my time there as one looks forward to reunion with a lover at day's end.

It was a meeting ground for me and my Muse, a playground, a chapel, a place where fears diminished and faithfulness grew. In the quiet and hollow of that near-empty space, a wonderful relationship was taking hold. Not out of some effort on my part, not as a result of striving or stretching toward that goal, but more surprisingly, it seemed, in the absence of effort. I was not, in that space, trying to achieve something, but simply to be. Expecting nothing, I found something.

This new presence stilled me, filled me, awakened a vitality that had long been dormant. When I created I felt I was no longer alone; as if, beside me, around me, within me, was a collaborator as intent as I to bring the inner out and the outer in. Out of the silence of that sacred space had risen a new voice, not mine, but ours.

Over time, as this connection deepened, I went less often to the sacred space, finding that the sacred stayed with me wherever I went. I could call on the Muse in crowded places, stepping into her quiet as if into a dream. I could walk by a river and feel her around me— I the water, and she the flow. She had become real, a companion, a force flowing through me like a mountain stream.

Looking back, I see now that it took the radical gesture of trans-

I have no parents—I make the heavens and earth my parents. I have no home—I make awareness my home.
—14th-century Samurai

From a certain inward strength arising from the acceptance of truth, we can build outward, majestically, transcendently, not by rising above things, but by rising to things.
—Manly P. Hall

Heaven is not a place nor a condition. It is merely an awareness of perfect oneness, and the knowledge that there is nothing else; nothing outside this oneness, and nothing else within.
—A Course in Miracles

forming that room to open myself for this new awareness: that any space is sacred the moment we declare it. It was not a lack of space that had hindered my creativity, but a lack of stillness and looking within. Before I could understand the significance of sacred space, I had to externalize it, act it out in life-size dimension. I needed to transform that space in order to prepare for my own transformation, to make it possible, to see what was needed.

As I stripped it of furniture and mundane accoutrements, I saw the need to cleanse my life of meaningless distractions. As I brought to the altar those things that I cherished, I noticed that all my senses were called into play, that the whole of me was needed for creative expression. And as I went back to the world from that place of calm and quiet, I learned the need to keep my center while I ventured to the edge.

That room is now a bedroom again, having served its time as sacred space. And when I sit at my computer, before I start, I say my prayers, open up, and strike a match to light the candle. To me, this is the sound of space becoming sacred.

Creating sacred space is the first step and, in many ways, the most important step in opening ourselves to the creative process. This is the gift we give to ourselves so that the multitude of gifts we are born to share have their own birthing place. It marks our commitment and symbolizes our readiness to serve and be served by the source itself.

Our space need not be large, but it needs to be defined, so that we are aware when we enter and leave it. If there are others in the household, they need to know it is as sacred as a sanctuary, not to be violated by noise or nattering. When you are there, for whatever time, you must be undisturbed, as if in prayer. And it is up to you to set these rules, to see that they are respected, to not capitulate to the inner voice that says you are not worth it, that others are more important.

If this troubles you, remember that the commandment is to love others *as you love yourself.* Love yourself fully then, that you may love others as well. This is your feeding time, your time to be nourished so you will have more to give when it is your time for giving. And the people in your life will respect you for this as they learn from your example how to better love themselves. And if, in their watching, they learn the value of inner time, perhaps they will get a glimpse of the magic that happens when we journey within.

Every time we walk down the street, we are preceded by hosts of angels singing, "Make way, make way, make way for the image of God."
—Rabbinic phrase

You are the whole ocean. Why send out for a sip of dew?
—Rumi

If the entire is to feed your soul, then in the littlest you must see the whole.
—Goethe

There are only two or three human stories and they go on repeating themselves as fiercely as if they had never happened.
—Willa Cather

As we retreat into the quiet of our inner being, open ourselves to the creative spirit, we are establishing conditions for the unimaginable to occur. When we bring to the threshold all we have and all we are— our time, our mindfulness, our desire to create— we are met by the Muse whose arms are full of gifts of her own. Gifts of words and sounds and visions that mingle with ours and become something new. Gifts of insight, flow, energy, freedom. Gifts of power for breaking through, breaking into, breaking out. Gifts of light, grace, wisdom, joy. She breathes her knowing into our doubt, casts her flame against our dark, offering all that she is asked, entering whenever invited.

When we create on this level, call on the spirit to infuse our work, we take part in a sacred event. It is worthy of reverence and jubilation, deserving of whatever your own heart calls for. As you make the space for this sacred dance, do it extravagantly, boldly, with flair and festivity. Remember, you are creating the space for a great adventure. Let it be worthy of the greatness to come.

Belief conditions experience, and experience then strengthens belief. What you believe, you experience.
—Krishnamurti

When Sleeping Beauty wakes up, she is almost fifty years old.
—Maxine Kumin

We are shaping history with our words. Either we speak as best we can or our power in relation will slip away like a thief in the night.
—Carter Heyward

Meditations and Actions

1. Put on some soothing music, light a candle, close your eyes, and imagine the space where you'll be meeting your Muse. Imagine her coming to visit you there, where she will be, where you will be, what things will surround you. Imagine bringing things into the space that inspire you. Imagine an altar there. What is on it? Imagine that there is nothing unessential in this space and that every detail is significant. Get a clear picture of it in your mind and make a list of what you'll need to get and get rid of and of what you need to do before you can use it. Give yourself a deadline for completion and commit some time every day toward preparing it.

2. Celebrate its opening with a fun ritual. Make a party to welcome the Muse. Blow up balloons. Light candles. Play music. Dance with her. Invite others who support you in your creativity to celebrate the opening. Or be there alone in the fullness of her

presence and quietly receive her gifts. She is your Muse. You will know by the time her space is ready exactly what to do. (As with all the suggestions in this book, they are meant only to start the ball rolling. The less literally you take any of them, the more you creative you will become as you invent your own rituals.)

3. Play the song "Tiny Geometrics" from *Deep Breakfast* by Ray Lynch. Light your candle and prepare for the Muse's entry. Imagine her arrival during this song. See what images occur, how she looks, what she wears, where she sits. Notice all the details. Hold them in your mind or write them down in your notebook. Do not stop to think about things. Write as fast as you can and only as long as the song lasts. Say everything you know and feel about her. See if she speaks to you, gives you anything, says her name. This is the beginning of one of the most important relationships in your life. Have fun!

Music Suggestions

Ray Lynch, *Deep Breakfast* (Windham Hill)
"Alleluia to Pachelbel Canon," *On Wings of Song and Robert Gass* (Spring Hill Music)
Mannheim Steamroller, *Fresh Aire* (any version I–VII; American Gramaphone Records)
Enya, *Shepherd Moons* (Reprise Records)
Chris Spheeris, *Electric Europe* (Columbia)
Paul Winter, *Wolf Eyes* (Living Music Records)
Vision: Music of Hildegarde von Bingen (Angel Records)
Wagner, Seattle Symphony, Gerard Schwartz (Delos International)
Parkening, *A Tribute to Segovia* (EMI Records)
Chip Davis, *Romance—Day Parts* (American Gramaphone Records)
Kitaro, *Silver Cloud* (Geffen Records)

Keeping the Journey Mind

We are each engaged in an epic journey, main characters in a modern-day *Odyssey* battling demons and dangers as we make our way home. We are weary with the fight, mostly alone, often lost. Our muscles are strained, and a hunger for what we can hardly name rises up from the hollow, but we keep on. When darkness arrives, we go to the hearth of the fire within, to that which is source and warming sustenance. When enemies emerge from the dark underside, we stave them off with valiant gestures, growing larger than the fear that grips us. In the face of danger, we do not retreat. We, the journeyers, are of pure intent, warriors of the light, each on a noble quest for the Holy Grail.

I try to remember this when the woman at the checkout counter brings twelve items to the five-items-only line, or when a driver cuts into my lane during rush hour traffic. But it's not a thought that stays fresh in my mind, not a concept that's supported by billboards or sound bites in the daily environment. I never hear messages like that when I need them, when I'm hurling blame and anger at others, so I play music that reminds me, read poems that place me nearer the heart of the other. I look to the arts to keep me mindful, not only of my own journey, but of the long, hard trek that my neighbors are on.

When the right music is playing, I see images of all of us together, trudging the darkened path, weary from the struggle, shuffling along hungry and cold, but not giving up. The image somehow comforts me, reminds me that we're all in it together, searching for the unseen, responding to the unknown.

On this road, at this time, we are common travelers, subject to similar fears and dangers, caught, so often, in the same nets. When I see that or remember that, I respond differently. I allow myself and others our flaws. When I'm in the journey mind, I find compassion moving closer to my surface, my hard edges softening, my judgments lightening.

But who speaks to us of our journey? Who helps us to frame our

Emily Dickinson never left her house after the age of thirty. Why should she leave? She was reinventing the world, she needed to stay in one place.
—*Jean Houston*

We are what we think. All that we are arises with our thoughts. With our thoughts we make the world.
—**Buddha**

All sorrows can be borne if you put them into a story or tell a story about them.
—*Isak Dinesen*

Eventually I saw that the path of the heart requires a full gesture, a degree of abandon that can be terrifying. Only then is it possible to achieve a sparkling metamorphosis.
—*Carlos Castaneda*

It is in the recognition of the genuine conditions of our lives that we gain strength to act and our motivation for change.
—*Simone de Beauvoir*

Live as you will have wished to have lived when you are dying.
—*Christian Furchtegott Gellert*

lives in this larger context as adventurers, warriors of a sort, on a quest for deeper knowing? How do we stay true to the journey, aware of our steps, mindful of the magnitude of our lives and the nature of our quest? How do we overcome the inertia and cultural conditioning of our times to place ourselves on the road as epic journeyers like Odysseus, who is, as Kazantzakis writes, "ample enough to contain the dualities without either resolving them into harmonious sterility or suffering an explosion of irreconcilable forces." Is it possible to speak to each other of this phenomenon, to rise above our ordinariness, look past our pettiness, and claim a certain connection to the heroic?

If I sat down next to someone in a K-Mart cafeteria and began to speak of our lives in terms of the great quest, the journey we have embarked upon, if I looked deep into her eyes and spoke with utmost sincerity, would she nod her head in understanding or call for security? I want to believe that she would understand, that on some deep and vaguely familiar level, she would find herself in the metaphor and be lifted up into a frame of reference outside the ordinary. That she would see herself defined, not only as a mother of three, a clerk in a convenience store, a wife, a Christian or Muslim or Jew—or any of those labels we were born or educated into—but also as a great spirit on a great adventure, choosing her own paths, following the direction of her own heart. And if she could see this and speak of it, I would cling to her words, find encouragement for my own journey, comfort that it feels the same to another as it does to me.

Carlos Castaneda says that the value of entering a nonordinary state, which is precisely what is needed to enter the journey mind, is to "exact what we need in order to embrace the stupendous character of ordinary reality." For him, the path of the heart is not a road of "incessant introspection or mystical flight, but a way of engaging the joys and sorrows of the world." It is a path into the depths, not out of them—a path that leads us to the truth behind our illusions, to the oneness that dwells behind our dualities.

When I was in my twenties, fresh out of the convent and trying to find my place in an alien culture of miniskirts, marijuana, and sexual liberation, I looked to the past for what was possible and took up waitressing, the only job I'd ever done before. I had no idea what to make of my life, and after saving some money, I headed west from upstate New York on a frantic search to find out who I was if I wasn't a nun.

I had no idea what to do, how to be, where to go, since I had planned from the age of twelve to be a sister and live in community. I had found my deepest joy there, found the ideal balance of prayer, solitude, community, and work. I had answered the call of the inner voice and found a life that was perfect for me, or so it seemed, until I was asked to leave after two years by superiors who decided I did not have a "religious disposition."

That was in the late sixties. For the next twenty years I crisscrossed the country, circumscribed the globe, on an epic journey to recover that joy I had known in community. I advanced from waitressing to clerk typist to social worker to a variety of other occupations, but always the longing was there, the hole in my heart that was never filled by what I was doing or where I was living. I wandered like a hermit in the desert, crying my questions into the night: What is it you will have me do? How is it you want me to serve? What path is mine and where shall I find it? Who am I to be? What am I to make of this life? Where do I look for my answers?

The grail I was seeking was that inner joy I had known at St. Joseph's Motherhouse, and in time I learned that the challenge of my journey was to create that joy in another context, in a culture that never felt quite right, never offered quite enough quiet, quite enough reverence for the life within.

I began to take what I found and make art of it, putting words, sounds, images together in a way that comforted and healed me. I made photographs I needed to see, wrote songs I needed sung to me. And words I needed to read, those I wrote, so that I would remember what I needed when loss and sadness rose up to meet me.

It was that artmaking that changed things, that mirrored me somehow, and gave me a vision of who I was and what I was here for. Creativity called for all the things the convent had called for—solitude, prayer, a sense of community, and a commitment to service. In order to create, I had to find that balance, and when I had it, joy returned. That joy I had always attributed to a place, a profession, eventually became available to me no matter where I was.

And now, nearly thirty years later, I see that the journeys I made in

If you follow your bliss, you put yourself on a kind of track, which has been there all the while waiting for you, and the life that you ought to be living is the one you are living.
—Joseph Campbell

If you have no anxiety, the risk you face is probably not worthy of you. Only risks you have outgrown don't frighten you.
—David Viscott

I do believe it is possible to create, even without ever writing a word or painting a picture, by simply molding one's inner life. And that too is a deed.
—Elly Hillesum

You draw from memory, from your understanding of life, and others' under-standing. All you've read and absorbed falls like a jewel into your being.
—*Martha Graham*

Now the real treasure, to end our misery and trials, is never far away; it is not to be sought in any distant region; it lies buried in the innermost recesses of our own home, that is to say, our own being. . . . But there is the odd and persistent fact that it is only after a faithful journey to a distant region, a foreign country, a strange land, that the meaning of the inner voice that is to guide our quest can be revealed to us.
—*Heinrich Zimmer*

my quest to discover this, the ones that were really important, were not the physical ones, but the metaphysical ones. The journeys into myself that were more about meaning than miles on a path. Journeys that started and ended with questions; questions that defined me, that gave shape to my life as we moved and danced and unfolded together. I am these questions I ask, as I am the journey I am on. There is no destina-tion except to become, as the flower in the garden whose destiny is to bloom.

The more aware we are of our journey, of the questions that propel us to the places where we arrive, the more we have a hand in shaping our lives. I read once that the sign of true wisdom is not an ability to know the right answers but to ask the right questions. I believe this, as I believe that wherever we are in our journey is related to the questions we have asked of ourselves, our gods, our universe.

My questions have led me here, to this writing, to this belief that if we express our journey in some way, try to share it with another, then we will understand it better, get it clearer in our focus and be awed by its beauty. And how ironic that while I'm writing this, the mail carrier comes and delivers two catalogs. One is from the Sisters of St. Joseph entitled *Portrait of a Journey*. It is a collection of artwork from sisters across the country. Their statement on the front cover reads:

> *Through the arts we contemplate and express the unity and holiness of all creation, and the heights and depths of the human heart in response to the great mysteries of existence. We affirm the power and prophecy of the arts and believe the arts to be an important ministry for hope and healing in a critical moment of world transformation.*

The second catalog is from the Institute of Noetic Sciences. It features their annual travel program, with this quote by Ursula Le Guin on the front: "It is good to have an end to journey towards; but it is the journey that matters in the end."

These things comfort me.

Meditations and Actions

1. Imagine you are viewing your life on a movie screen in a big theater. You are the hero of the film. What are the compelling conflicts you face? What goes into the decisions you make throughout the film? What or who is the antagonist? How did you end up in these circumstances? What will you do that is heroic? Will you applaud at the end?

2. Listen to "Pilgrim's Chorus" from the Wagner opera, *Tannhauser*. (Ultimate Opera, Collection 2, *Warner Classics Unlimited,* or available in your local library). Turn it up loud and be sure no one is around who will interrupt. Close your eyes and experience yourself as one of those pilgrims. When it is over, play it again. Allow yourself all the feelings that surface.

3. Get Adrienne Rich's book *Dreams of a Common Language* (W. W. Norton). Read it and give it to someone who comes to mind.

4. Listen to Kitaro's *Toward the West* or *Silk Road* (Geffen Records). Get in the journey mind, outside of time and place. While you listen, write about your own journey in your notebook—not trips that you've taken, but what grail you are seeking in your life. What noble challenge has your name on it? Who are you as a journeyer? What dangers do you face and which do you run from? Is anyone with you on the road? Do you see others out there on the journey? Do you have compassion for them? For yourself?

5. Light a candle. Put on your dance clothes. Play the song, "Rivers of Belief" from the CD *Enigma, MCMCC, A.D.* (Virgin Records). Dance the dance of your journey.

6. Watch the film *Beyond Rangoon* (Castle Rock Entertainment) with a friend who likes to talk about movies. Notice the journey the heroine is on and discuss the challenges and changes she goes through.

We have been socialized to respect fear more than our own needs for language and definition, and while we wait in silence for the final luxury of fearlessness, the weight of that silence will choke us. . . . The transformation of silence into language and action is an act of self-revelation and that always seems fraught with danger. We fear the very visibility without which we also cannot truly live . . . and that visibility which makes us most vulnerable is that which is also the source of our greatest strength.

Audre Lorde, *Sinister Wisdom*

Going First

For years, I went home for the holidays from all corners of the earth, spending hundreds of dollars and hours of time in transit, always with the greatest anticipation that this time my family would truly be all I wanted it to be. I had images of us in deep conversations, creating rituals that would become traditions passed down from generation to generation. I saw us sharing our spiritual journeys, speaking of our fears and transformations, laughing with great relief that we were all in a space safe enough to expose our vulnerabilities. I saw us reminding each other who we had been and sharing with each other who we were becoming and experiencing great joy at this revealing.

Year after year, I would board the bus or train or plane after days of family togetherness, disappointed that it never happened, that we had somehow missed the opportunity, denied ourselves the intimacy we all hungered for. I would firmly commit to never going back again, and every year I would return, always with the same hope. It recurred like a

And if we only declare what is wrong with us, what is our deepest need, then perhaps the despair and death will, in degrees, disappear.
—J. B. Priestly

bad dream until I finally understood one thing. Human beings, for the most part, are afraid to share what is deepest and most sacred in their lives. Afraid maybe of its inherent power, afraid of the risk that no one will care, afraid that we ourselves cannot even speak of such things without breaking down in tears, whether of sorrow or joy. So we hold it in, not even consciously, but simply because it's all we know to do to keep ourselves together.

A few years ago, I traveled around the United States interviewing people in small towns about their values, their faith, the meaning of their lives. I had no idea when I started how these people would respond to me, a total stranger, coming into their communities and asking questions I had no right to ask. What are you committed to? What values or moral codes do you live by, and where did you get them? What is the most powerful memory you have? Who inspired you most in your life and why? What do you do for comfort during the hard times? What is your image of God? What are your dreams, and what fears keep you from achieving them?

For some reason, I had to go a long way from home to begin something this intimate. Though I set out from Syracuse, New York, I to drive all the way to Lovingston, Virginia, before I had gathered enough courage for the first interview. Or more aptly, before I realized I had to start somewhere, despite my fear. I stopped at a diner and scanned the room, my eyes landing on a young man sitting alone in a booth. Hesitantly, I approached him and said that I was doing a story on people's values. I asked if I could sit down and ask him some questions about his life. He said yes, that he had a few minutes to spare. I brought out my notebook and a wrinkled sheet of legal paper that I had been writing questions on as I drove along, state after state.

I asked him the first question. "Who passed down values to you as a child, and what do you remember being told?" There was a long, quiet pause. He sipped his coffee, looked around the room, and said nothing. "Oh, boy, I knew this was bad idea," came the voice from within me. Then it occurred to me that maybe I should answer the question first, in order to show myself in some disarming way, like when the cowboy lays his guns on the table.

I told him the story of my mother saying to me, "When you walk down the street and pass by someone, always be sure to look in the eyes

All progress is inevitably accompanied by strife and shock. . . . Evolution never happens without work and suffering. It is not enough to let oneself be borne passively along by it; man must collaborate in the event.
—*Teilhard de Chardin*

Each of us treasures the places where we were taught best the nature of things.
—*Chaim Potok*

I am part and parcel of the whole and I cannot find God apart from the rest of humanity.
—*Mahatma Gandhi*

of that person and give them a big smile. You never know what kind of day they're having, and your smile could really make a big difference to them." I told him too that I still live by this and rarely pass by a person on the street without remembering my mother's words.

I cried a little as I talked about it, more touched by the sound of it than how it feels to do in real life. The quiet young man nodded his head slowly, and kept looking at me as if he knew exactly what I was talking about. Then he started talking, telling me how he used to write poems as a child and how his grandfather always encouraged him. "If God has given you a gift that you can give back to people," his grandfather said, "don't you ever turn your back on it. Whenever you feel a poem coming on, you sit down and write it. And after you write it, find some way to share it, because that's what God gave it to you for." He then recited this poem, which he held in his memory:

> In the stillness of the night
> when all things come to a close
> your mind fades into a world
> of its own
> Waves of thought crash along the shores of your mind
> while you overlook the sea of despair
> your heart fills with sorrow
> while your soul drowns with pity
> Slowly, slowly drifting through the darkness
> of sorrow wondering
> when the pain will ever end
> Walking through the rubbish of the past
> you stumble over the one thing you needed
> a place of hope, a place to rest
> a place to care, and a place
> you can call home.

It's not that it was the greatest poetry, but that he had written it, memorized it, and written it down so I could take it with me that was so touching. "I write when I get sad, then I feel pretty good after I write," he said. "I guess it's my way of crying. Your sadness has to come out one way or the other. People who can cry are the lucky ones."

What is important is not what hurts and pleases, but to see what is true. And then that truth will operate, not you.
—*Krishnamurti*

In any real good subject, one has only to probe deep enough to come to tears.
—*Edith Wharton*

Courage is the price life exacts for granting peace.
—*Amelia Earhart*

We stayed in that booth for an hour and a half, saying everything we could about who we were till he left for his job at the Waffle House across the road. Afterward, I sat there for quite awhile, dazed by the depths we had traveled together. In that short time, I had come to know so much of this man. Knew about his dad, a preacher man who was full of anger and used to hit him, almost killing him once; knew how he loved his grandfather, loved writing poetry but hardly did anymore, didn't know how to deal with his own anger, didn't want to drink but drank anyway, wanted to marry but didn't trust enough to love someone, thought a paid-for trailer and a two-year-old pickup were signs enough of success for him.

Sitting there in that red plastic booth, I felt a whoosh of gratitude run through my bones. That kind of intimacy does not occur by default. It has to be intended, worked at. It is countercultural, the opposite of how we learn to be with each other. We learn well to speak of the weather, to gossip about politicians and movie stars, to blame the government or the poor for what is wrong with our lives. We learn who is different and why they are threatening. We learn to stand in crowded elevators and speak not a word. We learn to cluster at bus stops and share nothing with one another. It is a cultural learning, born of a culture that fears intimacy as much as it fears difference and the challenges they offer.

I, along with everyone else, had learned who and why to fear. Now I was trying to get at something deeper: how to move through that fear, past those barriers of politics, color and culture, into the commonness I hoped we shared. The difficult part was to get beyond, not just my fear, but the judgments I made about people on first sight.

When I found myself in the home of an eighty-eight-year-old Kentucky man whose coffee table was littered with right-wing magazines and fundamentalist literature, I was afraid at first to let myself be known. We were too different. His world was too black and white, too rigid for me to fit into. What could I possibly learn from him? I thought he would hate me if he found out who I was and what I believed in. All the signs said we were each other's opposite, and after a few minutes in his living room, I knew this man and I had nothing in common.

My immediate response was to judge and disregard him. This was my cultural conditioning leading me to be as rigid as I judged him to

There is only one real deprivation, I decided this morning, and that is not to be able to give one's gift to those one loves most. . . . The gift turned inward, unable to be given, becomes a heavy burden, even sometimes a kind of poison. It is as though the flow of life were backed up.
—*May Sarton*

Fear is desire, not shame or guilt or inadequacy or any of those other things. The question to ask about fear is not what you are afraid of but what do you want. If you know what you want and you can have it, then fear doesn't seem like fear at all.
—*Jane Rule*

be. If I would give him a chance, go deeper than the surface, perhaps our likeness would emerge, perhaps we would find delightful similarities. But this possibility, the possibility of making a profound connection with a person who appears to be a polar opposite, is one that takes a great stretch of imagination.

I finally asked to have a talk with him. Cane in hand, he led me outside for a walk by the walnut trees. "I feed these walnuts to a squirrel friend who lives in that hollow locust tree over there," he said, pointing at the tree with his hand-carved cane.

"It's beyond comprehension how this walnut tree can produce a nut in such a short span of time that is so strong it takes a sledge hammer to crack it open. What's loose in this world that in one summertime can produce something like that?" He loved nature and had spent his life in the lumber business. The whole time we walked, he talked about trees, how he loved to be in their presence and listen to the wind rustle through their leaves, how he loved to watch things grow.

"I go to my garden, I plant a little grain of corn, and in three months' time, that little grain of corn has produced a big stalk with lots of blades, tassels, two or three ears of corn, and on each ear there's hundreds of little grains. Where does that power come from? Where does that kind of life come from?" He look around his land with the awe of a child in fairyland, then told me his greatest dream was to go west and see the redwoods.

After that walk, I was in love with Arthur Asher. Despite our differences, I had found his beauty, found the person that he really was beneath his beliefs and strange opinions. I sent him postcards of trees whenever I found one. "Dear Arthur, Go to the redwoods while there's still time. They are waiting for you. Love, Jan."

Months later when I returned home, there was a card from Arthur, a postcard of redwoods from the Sequoia National Park. "Dear Jan, I made it. They are so beautiful, they made me cry. Love, Arthur."

These are the possibilities that open up when we find our commonness with others. It doesn't take much, only daring to go first, speaking from our heart, asking about the other's. It is in that sharing, in that great risky leap of truth-telling, that others find in us not only our beauty, but a glimpse of their own.

We differ from others only in what we do and don't do—not in what we are.
—Anthony DeMello

When I have forgiven myself and remembered who I am, I will bless everyone and everything I see.
—A Course in Miracles

To live the symbolic life which the journey required so I could perceive it, I had to free myself from the encumbrance of the ordinary.
—Barbara Hammer

Meditations and Actions

1. Light the candle and put on some music. Consider the quote by Audre Lorde at the beginning of this chapter and respond to these questions in your notebook: What truths about yourself have you not made known to those you love and care about? What has kept you from sharing? In what ways might you be keeping others from sharing their deepest selves with you? How can you invite the people you care about to engage more deeply in your life? What people do you most enjoy being with? What characteristics do you most enjoy in them? Why? What kind of a listener are you? Do you ask others questions about their experiences or only report on your own? Do you surround yourself with people like yourself, or do you have friends who are different? Why?

2. Have a dinner party for one or more friends, and make it a point to share something about yourself you haven't shared before.

3. Start a conversation with a stranger in which you reveal something about yourself and learn something about the other.

4. Tell someone in your family what knowing them has meant to you.

5. Write a note to a childhood friend about an incident you both shared that still has an impact on your life.

6. Rent the video *Resurrection* (Universal Pictures), watch it with a friend, then talk about it over tea or a glass of wine.

Music Suggestions

Kitaro, *Live in America* (Geffen Records)

Vangelis, *Chariots of Fire* soundtrack (PolyGram Records)

Andres Segovia, *The Baroque Guitar* (MCA Classics)

Out of Africa soundtrack (MCA Records)

Chip Davis, *Dinner—Day Parts* (American Gramaphone Records)

Enya, *Memory of Trees* (Geffen Records)

Chris Spheeris, *Gallery* (Columbia)

Loreena McKennitt, *Winter Garden* (Warner Brothers)

Liz Story, *Escape of the Circus Ponies* (Windham Hill)

Daniel Kobialka, *Velvet Dreams* (Lisem Enterprises)

The Little Wise Ones

Whenever I talk to children about being artists, they know exactly what I mean. They don't need to be told they're artists. They already know it, and they can provide evidence on the spur of any moment, with whatever tools may be at hand.

Last summer when Annie and I were doing a writing retreat at one of my aunt's cabins in the Adirondacks, we were interrupted one morning by a knock on the door. Two of my young cousins had come to visit—Jamie, twelve, and Brittany, ten. I was working feverishly at the computer, and Annie was on the porch revising some personal essays. I told the girls that we were very busy writing, and they said they understood; they were writers, too.

They went on to explain. Oh yes, both of them had written a variety of short stories, Jamie wrote poetry and Brittany was working on a play for her friends. They knew all about the writing thing.

"Well then," I said, "won't you come in and write with us?" They joined us happily. The four of us talked for awhile about what they would work on, and they each decided to do a short story. The plan was to write for one hour, then take a lunch break and read the stories during lunch.

They chose their pads and pens carefully, then scanned the room for just the right spot. Jamie picked the flowered overstuffed chair with the wide wooden arms, plunked herself down, and immediately started filling up the pages of the purple pad with her story, "The Summer I'll Never Forget."

Brittany spread out belly down on the bed, knees bent and the soles of her pink sneakers facing the ceiling. Her number-two pencil was a perfect match for her yellow pad. In big bold letters she printed out at the top of the page, THE HALLOWEEN NIGHTMARE, then paused for a bit while she nibbled at the eraser and waited for the first sentence to come out of hiding.

I learned that you should feel when writing, not like Lord Byron on a mountain top, but like a child stringing beads in kindergarten—happy, absorbed, and quietly putting one bead on after another.
—Brenda Euland

To create means to relate. The root meaning of the word art is "to fit together" and we all do this every day. Not all of us are painters but we are all artists. Each time we fit things together, we are creating—whether it is to make a loaf of bread, a child, a day.
—Corita Kent

With Vivaldi stimulating our alpha waves and loons warbling in the background, the four of us worked at a steady pace in a lovely combination of solitude and togetherness. No one was in anyone's way. No words broke the necessary silence, and each was lost in the world she created. An hour passed in what felt like minutes.

I got up quietly and went to the kitchen to prepare our lunch, giving the writers a ten-minute warning. Heads nodded, but no one's attention left her work, and no hand paused on the legal pads. This was a writing frenzy if I had ever seen one.

When I finished making the sandwiches and warming up the soup, I called them to the table. Moans of regret came from everywhere.

"Oh no, I'm right in the middle of the most important part!"

"Can't we have just a few more minutes? Is that clock right? I can't believe a whole hour went by."

"Quiet, you guys, I'm working on an important paragraph!"

These were committed artists, so rapt in the joy of creative play that time to continue was all they craved. Food was too common a thing to pull them from the uncommon fun of making something up from nothing. We took a vote and decided to hold off lunch till the stories were finished.

When the last sentence was written, I dished up the soup as the writers made their way proudly to the dining-room table. We held hands and said grace, giving thanks for the time to write, to be together, and to share our stories. I asked who wanted to read first. Brittany said she did. While we sipped on soup and ate our egg-and-olive sandwiches, Brittany treated us to "The Halloween Nightmare," an exciting tale of intrigue and mystery about what happened to a young girl one Halloween night. It was unexpectedly funny, full of colorful details, imaginative, and hauntingly true. We clapped for Brittany, and each of us pointed out our favorite parts. She beamed with pride.

Then Jamie read her story of a summer adventure with her two best friends. It was seven pages long and delicately textured with prepubescent conflict, tension, and resolution. She too beamed when we applauded her writing and took time to discuss the details that made it work so well.

It was a touching event and one that I never anticipated when I heard the knock at the door. What I thought would be an interruption

---

There is nothing in the world that should not be expressed in such a way that an affectionate seven-year-old boy can see and understand it.
—*Leo Tolstoi*

Every child is an artist. The problem is how to remain an artist once he grows up.
—*Pablo Picasso*

Children, like animals, use all their senses to discover the world. Then artists come along and discover it the same way all over.
—*Eudora Welty*

A child's attitude toward everything is an artist's attitude.
—*Willa Cather*

turned out to be an inspiration. The girls were right to call themselves writers, and they didn't need anyone else to confirm it. Their writing was good because they did it for love, for the joy of visiting their imaginations, pulling out thoughts, and trying them on like clothes out of Grandma's closet.

Brittany and Jamie did not need a mentor calling forth their creativity as do many of us who have given up play as a daily practice. They had not forsaken that part of themselves where our deepest joy lives—the part that is of the heavens, that is in all of us, and that, while it is ours, belongs to the universe.

When I have the honor of talking to school children about making art, we talk about this part of ourselves. The part that's invisible but very strong, like electricity or love. They understand about their own uniqueness—how no one sees things in exactly the same way they do and so their art is never the same as anyone else's—and why that is good.

Children know these things while the rest of us need reminding. We have forgotten the importance of play, forgotten how not to compete, forgotten that the thing in us that makes us unique is precisely the thing we are here to express. That thing, which gives us the most joy, which we do to settle ourselves, and in which we find comfort and a certain peacefulness—is our art, the work we are called to do.

Kids nod their heads proudly when I speak of their uniqueness. They have a certain understanding about this. They are close to their creativity, best friends with their Muses, familiar with the power of imagination and playing in the imaginary.

In the matter of creating, they are, in fact, the wise ones.

No one has yet fully realized the wealth of sympathy, kindness and generosity hidden in the soul of a child. The effort of every true education should be to unlock that treasure.
—Emma Goldman

All children are artists, and it's an indictment of our culture that so many of them lose their creativity, their unfettered imaginations, as they grow older.
—Madeleine L'Engle

He knows himself greatly who never opposes his greatness.
—William Blake

Meditations and Actions

*What will bananas
look like in a million
years?
—Drew Gaebel, age
eight*

1. Set aside an hour to work on a creative project with a child. Assign each other the title of a short story to write, put on Vivaldi's *Four Seasons* (or whatever music the child chooses), and give yourselves a certain length of time to write the story. At the end of that time, allow a few minutes to wrap it up, and then read your stories to each other. Have a conversation about the stories and comment on your favorite parts of each one.

2. This one you can do alone or with kindred spirits of any age: Get a sketch pad with large-size paper (at least eleven by fourteen inches). Using crayons, watercolors, colored pencils, or chalks, create a map of your life in three segments, including where you came from, where you are, and where you are headed. Take some time to explain your maps to each other.

3. Listen to the song "Children" on Sweet Honey and the Rock's *Good News* (Flying Fish Records). Following the song, take your notebook and write two pages without stopping on what images and feelings the song brings to mind.

4. Set aside one day to be orchestrated by a child. From morning till evening, the child will direct all activities, including travel (within a prescribed radius), meals, and entertainment. This may need to be planned in advance in order to budget for it. At the end of the day, talk about what happened, how it felt, what you liked. Thank each other for your company and go get a good night's sleep.

5. Write yourself a letter from yourself at the age of eight. Talk about what interests you, who your friends are and what they're like, what you hope to do when you get bigger, what your mom and dad are like. Get into the feeling of being eight and see how it feels.

Music Suggestions

Nigel Kennedy, Vivaldi, *The Four Seasons* (EMI Records)

Paul Winter, *Sunweaver* (Living Music Records)

Ray Lynch, *Nothing Above My Shoulders But the Evening* (Ray Lynch
    Productions)

Best of Tchaikovsky (Philips)

Also Sprach Zarathustra—Richard Strauss, Andre Previn and the
    Vienna Philharmonic (Telarc International)

Narada Collection, *Celtic Spirit* (Narada)

Loreena McKennitt, *The Mask and the Mirror* (Warner Brothers)

Windham Hill, *Piano Sampler 1* (Windham Hill)

Constance Denby, *Novus Magnificat* (Narada)

A Deeper Kind of Seeing

Five years ago I lived in a farming community in northern New York whose claim to fame was that it was home to more cows than people. It was also home to an Amish settlement of seventy-five families who had migrated from Pennsylvania in search of cheaper land.

I drove by their pristine farms regularly on my beat as photographer for the *Gouverneur Tribune Press*, scanning the countryside for front-page feature photos. Though I was bound by honor not to photograph the Amish, I loved to look and hungered for an opening into their lives, a chance to capture on film some fragments of a culture so unlike my own. It gnawed at me, this hunger, as I passed by their homes, the most beautiful scenes in the county. On the Amish farms, there were no rusted cars or trucks in the yards, no electrical lines jutting into the frame, no piles of garbage or caved-in outbuildings. Each farm was a calendar image, painted by an artist with an eye for detail, everything in its place, every color coordinated.

One day when I went to an Amish mill to buy some lumber, a young boy led me to the tack room in the barn where his father was repairing harnesses for the horses. It was a dark room with a single shaft of light streaming through the window. The smell of leather saturated the air, and rows of bridles hung from the ceiling in perfect order, their silver bits glistening in the golden light.

The Amish never stopped what they were doing until they were finished, so I stood in the dimness like an unnoticed guest. The man reached for his tools with a surgeon's precision and, hovering over the old black anvil, hammered and shaped each bit into place. While sweat stains darkened his tattered blue shirt and dust specks danced in the stream of gold light, I felt for a moment transported in time, lost in an image from ages ago.

Whenever I did business with the Amish, which was as often as possible, I loved the sense of timelessness and other-worldliness I felt

I often see through things right to the apparition itself.
—Grace Paley

The role of the artist I now understood as that of revealing through the world-surfaces the implicit forms of the soul, and the great agent to assist the artist was the myth.
—Joseph Campbell

Where thou art, that is Home.
—Emily Dickinson

when I was among them. I was happy to wait when other customers were ahead of me, grateful for the chance to linger and pretend. In my mind's eye, I'd frame shots, imagining the day I'd be invited in and allowed to photograph, once they understood that my intentions were pure.

Though I raced like Andretti through the rest of the county, I slowed to a crawl when I reached the settlement. Driving through Amish country was like driving through a dream. Tractors didn't roar down the furrowed fields, nor did balers and combines churn through the meadows. Harnessed for work, mules brayed out their complaints, while horses snorted and pranced down the two-lane roads, pulling steel-wheeled buggies overflowing with children. Clotheslines swayed in the midday breeze, as blue trousers and work shirts flapped against the wind. They were sounds and sights of another time, a different culture, foreign to my senses, and so intriguing.

One night I heard on the news that a drunk driver had run into a buggy and two children were rushed to the hospital with broken bones. Everyone knew the Amish weren't insured. They didn't traffic much in the world of cash, and there was no telling how they'd be able to cover their medical bills.

The next morning I drove to the nearest Amish farm and inquired about the Yoder family. I explained that I was a photographer for the newspaper and thought we could raise some money for the family if we did a story on them. The woman was friendly and appreciative but said I would need to speak to the bishop about getting permission. He lived three farms down.

I knocked on the screen door and a young woman answered. When I asked for the bishop she invited me in, then went to fetch him. The room was stark, with bare floors and walls and a few wooden straight chairs in no apparent order. Three young curly-haired children peered out from the kitchen doorway, then a short stocky man with a salt-and-pepper beard walked into the room. With an odd kind of accent he announced that he was the bishop and asked what I wanted.

I said that I had heard the news about the Yoder family's accident and wondered if it would be possible to do a story for the newspaper, take some photographs, and raise some money to help with their medical expenses. While I was talking, the bishop looked over my

---

Wakefulness is a state of non-illusion where you see things not as you are but as they are.
—Anthony DeMello

Not to transmit an experience is to betray it.
—Elie Wiesel

Hope is a very unruly emotion.
—Gloria Steinem

Great imaginations are apt to work from hints and suggestions, and a single moment of emotion is sometimes sufficient to create a masterpiece.
—Margaret Sackville

shoulder out the window, fiddled with a gold watch that dangled from a chain on his black vest, and nodded his head until I was done.

This would not be possible, he said, because his people did not want interference from the outside. "We have come here to practice our faith and to live our lives in privacy, away from the rest of the world." He reminded me that they do not allow photographs and were not interested in any newspaper article. "This is our religious belief and you will honor it." The patriarch had spoken.

I had not realized how high my hopes were until I felt them dashed to pieces. While I wanted to respect this man's wishes, I wanted even more to get my way, to get permission to photograph a piece of this exotic world and, in the process, generate support for a family in need. I appealed again.

"Bishop, you have no idea how hard it is to go by these farms every day and not be able to photograph. I check my values against these scenes. I reflect more deeply on my own faith every time I pass a buggy or see a barn raising. I learn from your community even though I am not a part of it, and it is hard to accept that you will not allow me to do this story. "Well, then," he said, "it is you who needs the help, not the Yoder family. We will do fine without you. Now, if you would please leave."

He opened the screen door. I thanked him and walked out, disheartened and embarrassed. I drove more slowly than ever that day, taking in as much as I could, now that the illusion was gone of someday being able to photograph there. I could never capture a moment for later reference, never borrow even a fraction of a second from the lives of these people, not for the newspaper, not for the Yoder family, not to add beauty to my walls, or to help me stay clear on my own path to simplicity.

Now, whatever it was that touched me about this community, whatever magic moved me to think differently, even to feel and be different while I was there, that power I would have to absorb into myself. The images that I could not capture on film would have to be recorded in the place of deepest memory where I could save them for times when I needed to remember.

When I heard the clippety-clop of hooves behind me, I pulled to the side of the road, opened the window, and turned back to watch the approaching buggy make its way toward me like a slow-motion movie sequence. I studied the freckled faces of the curly-haired children, smiled

Think of all the beauty still left around you and be happy.
—Anne Frank

Our visions begin with our desires.
—Audre Lorde

To look at oneself without any judgment is of the greatest importance, because that is the only way you can understand and know about yourself.
—Krishnamurti

The assumption of being an individual is our greatest limitation.
—Pir Vilayat Khan

Every part of this earth is sacred to my people. Every shining pine needle, every sandy shore, every mist in the dark woods, every clearing and humming insect is holy in the memory and experience of my people.
—*Chief Seattle*

at the young mother as she flicked the reins and made the old familiar clicking sound with her tongue that all horses know means, "Keep going, fella!" As the cirrus clouds streaked eastward in the light-blue sky, smells of freshly-mown hay drifted through the countryside. Two children across the road wrestled for the best seat on an old tire swing while a young boy in a straw hat hitched a team of horses for their stint in the fields. Out there in an apron was Mrs. Yancy at her roadside stand making change for Homer Henshaw, who drove in twice a week from DeKalb Junction for her rye bread and pecan pies.

Who knows, maybe I would have missed these things if I had been photographing. Maybe I wouldn't have had to breathe it in so deeply, knowing I could shoot now and view later, like a tourist in a foreign land who gets everything on film but misses the experience. Maybe if I hadn't had that talk with the bishop, everything would have been different. But something shifted that day and my whole way of looking changed. Once the craving was gone—that awful temptation to photo-graph what I had no right to—I was, in a way, freed up. I abandoned the fantasy of framing this world in my telephoto lens, and my vision of it expanded along with my ability to appreciate and absorb it.

I learned to savor every detail, every color, smell, and sound. I couldn't be a tourist there, invading their lives. I was a neighbor. I could drive by any time I wanted a refresher course in simplicity, walk through any time I craved the balance that contrast provided. I had the real thing in my own back yard. I didn't need an eight-by-ten hanging on my wall.

The bishop was right. I did need more help than the Yoders. I needed to learn how to satisfy my longing in another way, even to understand what that longing was about. What intrigued me about the Amish was not just the surface—not just the clothing, the buggies, the old tools, the straw hats—although those elements all held a certain photographic appeal.

The real draw was what happened inside me when I was in the presence of that differentness. How being in a house lit by lanterns made me think differently about my use of energy, how watching an Amish community barn raising made me reflect on the lack of commu-nity in my own life. The resourcefulness of the Amish shone a light on my extravagance. Their simplicity exposed the uselessness of many of my distractions. Contrasts like that startle the brain. They stir up new thoughts, as does any venture into an unknown culture, as we imagine ourselves living out new traditions, bound by different rules, or feeling, perhaps, the holes in our lives that some part of the other culture might be able to fill. And always, we return to the familiar somewhat altered by whatever transpired in the course of our musings.

I hold those memories inside me as if I were sitting even now in the rocker on the porch, next to the mother as she stitches patches on her baby's quilt, drawing the needle in and out, in and out.

Meditations and Actions

1. Go to your library and take out the book or audio tape *Plain and Simple* (Harper and Row) by Sue Bender. Share it with a friend. Once you've both read it, prepare a simple meal together and make *Plain and Simple* the subject of your dinner conversation.

2. In your journal, list all the reasons you take photographs. Then write down what you do with the photographs after they are processed. Do you put them in an album? Write captions of what is going on? Do you share them with people? Do you ever give them away? Do you throw away the fuzzy ones with the big blur of your finger in front of the lens?

3. Gather together as many photos as you can find from your childhood. Sit with them for awhile and let whatever stories come up take your attention. Take fifteen to twenty sheets of paper and select fifteen to twenty photographs that have some meaning. Attach one photo to the top of each sheet. After reflecting on the image for a while, write a story about what is going on in that picture. Try to get back into your head at the time the picture was taken, and create a narrative that describes something essential about who you were then. Put the images in chronological order and write something about each photograph, ending with a picture that is contemporary. Put these all in a

notebook and think of it as your first autobiography. Write an introduction and epilogue, and share it with your friends.

4. Walk around your neighborhood as if you were seeing it for the first time. Imagine that an entirely different culture is in place there and that you have come in from another country. Notice what things people have in their yards, on their porches, on their flagpoles. What can you tell about any of them from noticing these accoutrements? What might someone know about you from what your yard/house looks like?

Music Suggestions

Michael Jones, *Touch* (Narada)
Anonymous Four, *Miracles of Santiago* (Harmonia Mundi)
Benedictine Monks of Santo Domingo de Silos, *Easter Chants* (Milan Records)
Kitaro, *In Person* (Domo Records)
John Williams, *Spanish Guitar Favorites* (MCA Classics)
Enya, *The Celts* (Reprise Records)

A woman came to Paris to stand on a bridge after dreaming she would get help for her sick children. They had a dangerous disease, and she had no money for medicine. In her dream, she learned that she might save them by standing on a bridge every Thursday. One night while she was standing on the bridge for the third time, a merchant passed by. Hearing her story, he laughed at her simplicity. "I have also been dreaming; I dreamt that I dug under the tree in park yonder and found a lot of gold. But I don't believe in dreams." Scornful, he went away. The woman went to the nearest inn, borrowed a spade, and started to dig. Soon she found gold and was able to buy medicine, and her children were cured of their disease.

Medieval fairy tale

Believing in the Dream

While on the bridge for the third time—that's the line I'm taking from this story for today's mantra. How many times I have given up on a dream or a project because all the pieces didn't come together on the first try. I have filing cabinets full of good starts, half-written stories, beautiful photo essays, all abandoned because they were rejected by one publisher. I know better, literally, but it takes a particular wisdom and inner stamina to keep pursuing our projects when they are rejected by people with publishing power.

When I use the word *power* in this matter, I am not talking about *authentic* power, original power, as in our power to create, to love, to

One certainty we all accept is the condition of being uncertain and insecure.
—Doris Lessing

heal. I am referring to *commercial* power, the power of those with the last word in today's ever-growing media monopoly. Dealing with this kind of power is one of the great challenges for those of us creating and seeking outlets for our work.

I have a friend who is an executive at a multinational media corporation with a book-of-the-month club. Six years ago, when my book *Making Peace* was published, she said she would look at it to see if she could "do anything with it." The book is full of photographs and stories of the transformation I went through personally, spiritually, and politically during an eighteen-month peace pilgrimage around the world.

After reading it, she wrote me a lovely letter saying that she personally loved the book but that, unfortunately, people were not interested in spiritual journeys. "That kind of thing doesn't sell," she wrote. In the next paragraph, she referred to the multimillion dollar budget she was overseeing for the celebration of Bugs Bunny's fiftieth anniversary.

I couldn't argue with her. She knew her audience. Back then maybe people weren't interested in the spiritual path like they are today. But I couldn't help wondering if they would be if they were exposed to it and given a choice. If you offer starving people cotton candy, they will eat it willingly, but that doesn't mean they wouldn't prefer bread.

If my commitment as a creative person was to produce only material that sells in this culture, I would have to abandon many of my projects. My motivation, fortunately, is not so much to write what will sell as to write what I want to give to the world. If I do it well enough, speak it clearly enough, it will be art worthy of publication.

As I write this now, I have no evidence that these words will see the light of day, and yet I give it my time because I believe in it. Because it calls me from my bed. It wakes me up. It holds me and does not let me go.

This compilation of words, images, dreams, this piece of art, now with its own life, calls on me to believe in it. And I do. And when you read it one day, you will see for yourself how it happens. The piece starts with an impulse to share, builds into a body of work, takes on its own energy, and finds its way to the world.

The hardest part for most of us is to stay true to the impulse, the original idea. I once had an idea for a book of interviews with artists

In the creative state, a man is taken out of himself. He lets down as it were a bucket into his subconscious, and draws up something which is normally beyond his reach. He mixes this thing with his normal experience and out of the mixture he makes his work of art.
—*E. M. Forster*

Dreams pass into the reality of action. From the action stems the dream again; and this interdependence produces the highest form of living.
—*Anaïs Nin*

You must do the thing you think you cannot do.
—*Eleanor Roosevelt*

who were creating work that said something about the world we live in, art with a sense of social consciousness about it. I had my artists all lined up and a pretty good sense of the look and feel of the book. I had produced a few chapters and done some interviews when the opportunity came up to meet a literary agent who was giving a workshop on writing book proposals.

When I raised my hand to ask a question, she asked what kind of book I was working on. I told her what I had in mind, and she said, "Oh, that won't sell. Publishers aren't interested in interview books." That's all, dismissed. Then she went on to someone else's question. One person, one opinion, one short sentence from a total stranger was enough for me to abandon the whole project.

Weeks later, I visited my Uncle Roger in the hospital before his heart surgery. He himself was a man of dreams, a lover of life, a poet and philosopher. He knew I'd been working on this book and asked how it was going. "I'm not doing it," I told him. "I talked with an agent and she said publishers weren't interested in that kind of material."

He scrunched up his forehead and shook his head back and forth. "It's not your job to worry about publishers," he said. "You're a writer. Write your book and it will find its own way out."

Something shifted for me when he said that, so matter-of-factly. He was right. As an artist, it is not my job to wait for all the pieces to come together before I write. My job is to write, to give shape to whatever it is that whispers from within.

I know this is a departure from traditional thinking. I have read all those books and magazine articles that say, don't write the piece until you have a commitment, don't waste your time on something you can't sell. And I think if you are trying to make a living at your craft, perhaps there is some wisdom in that. But I don't want my creativity to be bound. I want more freedom. I want to work on things I love for their own sake, for my sake. I'd rather create out of love and passion with no regard for what's to become of the piece than to hold up the process until I have some certainty that somebody wants it.

The man on the bridge had no time for dreams. He was interested in what is and scorned the woman for believing in what might be. He was like the literary agent who said, this is how it is, no one will want it. She was like my Uncle Roger who said to follow your instincts, you never

Art always has something of the Unconscious about it.
—D. T. Suzuki

If you pay attention to your dreams, they will begin to speak to you.
—Natalie Goldberg

There is something else which has the power to awaken us to the truth. It is the works of writers of genius. . . . They give us, in the guise of fiction, some-thing equivalent to the actual density of the real, that density which life offers us every day but which we are unable to grasp because we are amusing ourselves with lies.
—Simone Weil

know what will happen. Oddly enough, it was in the man's cast-off dream that she found her answer. Had he believed in his own dream, he would have been all the richer.

The more we listen to the messages we get from life, both inner and outer, the closer we come to finding our riches. Our clues come from everywhere: from our own and each other's dreams and creations, from nature, from our children and our animals and our prayers and our ponderings.

What we need to know, we already know. It is not more knowledge that is needed, but more careful listening, more dreaming, more daring. It is believing in the possibility that the voice within our skin has an answer to someone else's question, if not our own.

I find most of my insights in other people's creations. I'm stirred by their writings, their music and art, and I respond by creating something of my own. It's an organic thing, like art birthing art on a more cosmic level. It is coming at our work from the bottom up rather than from the top down.

I dream. I wake up. I pay attention to the images, the feelings of the dream. I listen for the inner voice. I wait to see if there is something there wanting more expression. I go through my day, mindful and attentive to what draws me in. I pay attention to my thoughts, regard those things that recur in waking and dreaming hours. I go through more days like this, and then one day it creeps into consciousness— what wants to be created starts to take shape and nudge at my brain. It already has its own life. I do not have to worry about what to create, only how to let it out.

It is not my job to worry how this piece will find its way into the world. It is my job to be open, to let it flow, to breathe it in and out. To write the words, one after another, as the spirit moves. To keep believing, as did the dreamer—on the bridge, for the third time.

Dreams are illustrations . . . from the book your soul is writing about you.
—Marsha Norman

When you dream, you dialogue with aspects of yourself that normally are not with you in the daytime and you discover you know a great deal more than you thought you did.
—Toni Cade Bambara

Meditations and Actions

1. In your notebook, list the times in your life you have been or felt rejected. Next to each one, write what you did in response. Notice how you tend to react. See if your confidence in your work wavers if others do not approve of it. Have you completed any creative projects for your own benefit alone, just for the sake of creating? What was it that compelled you? If not, what gets in the way?

2. Make a deal with a few friends to keep a dream journal for one month. At the end of the month, come together with your journals and share your dreams. See if you find any insights, answers, or clues about life in each other's dreams. Keep it up if it feels good.

3. Make two lists: The Worst Thing Someone Could Say about My Work and The Best Thing Someone Could Say about My Work. What it is you want to be recognized for? What is the criticism you fear? What matters most to you about either one? What do you love so much that you would never stop doing it no matter what anyone said? What keeps you from making this your life work?

4. Light the candle and put on some peaceful music. Invite your Muse for a conversation. Tell her about an experience in your life that you would like to translate into another form. Talk about your ideas for awhile and then take some time to listen. You may want to have your notebook open so you can write down the thoughts she'll be adding to your idea.

5. Get together with a few other artists and see what you can do to publish or present your work as a group. (Chapbooks are easy and affordable to self-publish; banks and restaurants are often eager to exhibit the work of local artists; schools often look for visiting artists and writers to share and talk about their work).

It is in our idleness, in our dreams, that the submerged truth sometimes comes to the top.
—*Virginia Woolf*

Most successful people are unhappy. That's why they are successes—they have to reassure themselves about themselves by achieving something that the world will notice. . . . The happy people are failures because they are on such good terms with themselves that they don't give a damn.
—*Agatha Christie*

Remember, you do not have to rely on a publisher or gallery to get your work seen and heard.

6. Identify a person in whose presence you feel most alive. What is it about her/him that calls this forth in you? What are the circumstances in which you feel this way? What is the environment that most nurtures you? What can you do to create it on a more regular basis?

7. Rent the video *Babe*. Have a couple friends over, eat popcorn, have fun.

Music Suggestions

Chip Davis, *Impressions* (American Gramaphone Records)
Paul Winter, *Common Ground* (Living Music Records)
Narada, *The Wilderness Collection* (Narada)
Music for Lute, Guitar and Mandolin (VOX Music)
Christopher Parkening Plays Vivaldi (EMI Records)
Andres Segovia, *My Favorite Works* (MCA Classics)

The Art of Activism

About every third day I find the courage to pick up a newspaper. Over the past year, I've noticed myself giving it up, section by section. Curious, since I've always prided myself on being informed, always enjoyed the excitement of a political conversation, had a handle on the latest uprisings in every country, and could explain my version of world politics in a way that any fifth-grader could easily grasp. I thrived on it.

If someone had asked me to describe myself one short decade ago, I would have said "social activist" in less than a heartbeat. Social activism was, for me, the clearest way to act out my spiritual life. It was the closest I could come to living out my prayers, a good antidote for powerlessness, and a way of practicing my belief that, on some level beneath the surface of our lives, we are all connected and responsible for each other.

It took no stretch of the imagination to go to bat for nuclear disarmament, to march in the streets for human rights, or to demonstrate against racism. It was a privilege to work for next to nothing in an organization that published artwork promoting peace, ecology, and human kindness; an honor to travel all night in a crowded bus to wrap a twelve-mile peace ribbon around the Pentagon or to attend local rallies for political prisoners in Central America and Eastern Europe.

I did not have to work at seeing the connection between their lives and mine, for that had been trained into me at an early age—by the church that taught me I was my sister's and brother's keeper, by my mother who taught me never to pass up an opportunity to be of service to people, and by a few gifted teachers who set my heart on fire with a passion for justice.

It was not as if there was a formal curriculum being offered by mentors on my path. There was nothing so clear as a defined career track in social activism. Those of us who ended up there made it up as we went along, choosing the freedom of immediate response over the tyranny of time clocks, and trading the comforts of material wealth for the luxury of

What you will do matters. All you need is to do it.
—Judy Grahn

We're all born into this mess. We're not responsible for it. We're only responsible for every day we let it go on without changing things.
—Gloria Steinem

Participate with joy in the sorrows of the world.
—Buddhist principle

We save the world by being alive ourselves.
—Joseph Campbell

doing what we wanted with the time of our lives.

With no less than the world in our scope, we did what we could to help shape a future of fairness and honor. We lived as if the world counted on us, as if every action mattered, as if even our thoughts had weight. It was a time of acute attentiveness. We scanned the globe for signs of injustice and mobilized our forces to fight against it. From our own neighborhoods to Namibia, if there was something wrong, we set out to right it in whatever way our means would allow.

Over the years, my attention has shifted from the outer to the inner. I notice that I shy away from the painful details of global conflict, skip the story if the headline seems too brutal, no longer initiate conversations about oppression here or repression there. It is not that these things do not enter into me, not that I live in some state of nirvana, unaware of the tragedy of our times, of the awful toll that greed and violence take on the human spirit. Like poison in the air, this awareness seeps into me and colors everything I do.

Whatever art I make contains my knowledge of the world. It is informed by what enters me, which in turn is transformed by that which is deep within me. In the mingling of these elements—what I know and what I dream—some new form takes shape, some new thought, perhaps, that will add to the collective consciousness; that could, in fact, be the mystifying random proton that shakes it up, shifts the gears, and propels us forward on our search for solutions.

Art has this power. It is a critical complement to activism, lending soul to a function that is often brain-heavy and spirit-thin. No matter how brilliant our attempts to inform, it is our ability to inspire that will turn the tides.

People are not, for the most part, moved to action by written information. People are moved by music, by images that touch the common center, by other people whose lives are full and joyous. When I look for hope, I turn to the arts, to the symbols and images that heal and nudge. Not to the mainstream cultural centers where I rarely find values that reflect my own, but to work being produced by artists who are addressing the richness, the sacredness, and the crisis of the contemporary human family.

I'm inspired by work that relates matter to spirit, that transforms a chunk of honest reality into profound possibility by a change of tone or

The creation of a thousand forests is in one acorn.
—*Ralph Waldo Emerson*

Living is a form of not being sure, not knowing what next or how. The moment you know how, you begin to die a little. The artist never really knows. We guess. We may be wrong, but we take leap after leap in the dark.
—*Agnes deMille*

The question of bread for myself is a material question, but the question of bread for my neighbor is a spiritual question.
—*Nikolai Berdyaev*

throw of light. I'm inspired by the power of intimacy, so images of strong, tender women cover my walls and lift me up. I'm inspired by new icons, symbols of a spirituality that is beyond religion, crucial to my politics, and the basis for my creative work.

Art, though it often heals the artist, has a power more universal than personal. Art created with a sense of integrity has a redemptive power, a healing power that helps us transcend the tragic particularities of our culture. Art created from a sense of commitment tells the truth about our world, concerns itself with people rather than profit, aims to upset the standards that rank one class, one race, one country above another.

Let us, in our creative work, summon new thought, envision a future that has every one of us wrapped in its arms, safe, warm, and well fed. And then, having envisioned it, let us give it shape in our poetry, our paintings, our songs, and our sculptures. Let us breathe out into the world an art that bears witness to the triumph of our sensibilities and helps us remember what we need to remember in order to survive.

Meditations and Actions

1. Imagine one kind act you could perform for a neighbor and do it.

2. Clean out your closets and remove everything you haven't worn in the past year, including shoes and coats. Think about giving away the items you haven't used. Listen to the reasons you state for needing to keep them. Compare your reasons to the needs of a person who is homeless or poor and who may need the things you no longer use. Do whatever you want with your clothes.

3. Enlist some of your friends in the same process.

4. Create a piece of art that says something about finding ourselves in each other. It could be a poem, a drawing, a short story. Give it to a person in whom you have seen yourself reflected in some way.

5. Finish the sentence, "If I could do one thing to improve my neigh-

When the world becomes repressive and ugly and mean, we need form and beauty and balance and music—that's when artists feel most pressed into service.
—Dorianne Laux

If we get cut off from our passion, where's our compassion going to come from?
—Matthew Fox

The art of writing has for backbone some fierce attachment to an idea.
—Virginia Woolf

To be great, art has to point somewhere.
—Anne Lamott

borhood, I'd . . ." Talk to two of your neighbors about this and see if they share your concern. Find out what they would like to do. Agree on a plan of action to make one positive contribution to your neighborhood within the year.

6. Give blood to the Red Cross.

How can one not speak about war, poverty, and inequality when people who suffer from these afflictions don't have a voice to speak?
—*Isabel Allende*

The artists are on the opposite side of whatever may lead to destruction, and once they set themselves steadily to fulfill their mission, all systems of politics and social order are in some jeopardy.
—*Harold Taylor*

What we do with our lives individually is not what determines whether we are a success or not. What determines whether we are a success is how we have affected the lives of others.
—*Albert Schweitzer*

Stretching the Boundaries of Creativity

Whenever the subject of creativity comes up, there's always someone who says, "I'm not creative. I can't even draw stick figures," as if creativity is all about drawing. Somewhere along the path, most of us have picked up the fallacy that creativity is an attribute of only a chosen few, and if we don't produce artistic or painterly things, we are probably not creative.

My hope in writing this book is not that more people will sign up for drawing classes or set about improving their skills in an artistic medium so they can squeeze into an elite class of "creative people." My hope is to expand the definition of creativity so that more of us—all of us—can begin to perceive ourselves as creators, to pay attention to what rises up from our depths in response to our daily experiences, and to do something with it to communicate on some level, in some form, what we notice occurring between our inner world and our outer world.

Whether this action results in a poem, a painting, or an intimate conversation with someone we trust, the act of giving words to the previously unspoken is itself a creative act. It is a noble gesture—one of giving honor to the elements of our lives. I have these thoughts; here is a poem I made with them. I carry this image in my mind; here is a crayon drawing of what it looks like to me. I have these fears; this is a story I wrote to help me sort them out. To be engaged with our lives on this level is magical. It allows us to see ourselves as actors in the drama, to take part in the creation of our own lives and move in the direction our spirit is calling us.

The other day I read an article by psychologist and philosopher Jean Houston in the *Noetic Sciences Review*. At first it seemed so dense I could barely wade through it, but there were sentences here and there that made my heart leap, ideas that felt at once totally new yet profoundly familiar.

Farmer Haggett knew that little ideas that tickled and nagged and refused to go away should never be ignored, for in them lie the seeds of destiny.
—*From the movie,* **Babe**

Your work is to discover your work and then with all your heart to give yourself to it.
—*Buddha*

The article is on the subject of *entelechy*, which is from a Greek word that means the dynamic, purposeful unfolding of what we are. Entelechy is that which "propels us to actualize our essence," Houston writes. "It is the entelechy of an acorn to be an oak tree; the entelechy of a baby to be a grown-up human being." Some of us have the experience of sensing at an early age what we are destined to become, but many of us find ourselves middle aged and still wondering what we are supposed to be when we grow up.

Of all the educational training we receive in this country, little attention is focused on tuning into our essential selves and letting that essence lead us into the future. I hear high school students saying they want to be doctors so they can be rich or lawyers so they can be like the stars on *Law and Order*. It's an "I'm going to do this so I can get that" motivation rather than a response to a passion they feel in their bones. What's tragic about this is not that these young ones don't have passion, but that they get so little assistance in finding and articulating it. We have the army's "Be All That You Can Be" recruiting slogan and Nike's "Just Do It" campaign, but who do we have out there saying this is *how* you can be it and do it, this is *how* you get at your passion and *how* you tune into your inner voice?

I craved that kind of attention when I was young. I longed for someone to talk to me about what was possible, about who I was and what I could do, and about the vast unfolding universe of which I was somehow an important, though tiny, part. My mother did this in small ways, but she was confined by her culture and her role of keeping us in line. And she herself was never coached in finding her essence. Her programming was to find out what needed doing and then do it.

When I was in sixth grade, I was extremely shy and lived quietly in my own little cocoon. I never spoke out in class, had only one friend, and never exuded much of a personality. I was afraid no one would like me and didn't think I had much to offer. My teacher, Sister Helen Charles, took me on like a project. She saw some potential in there somewhere and started a positive reinforcement campaign with a vengeance. Though it now seems unfair to the rest of the class, she singled me out as her shining star, called on me constantly, had me do special jobs for her after class, named me the official "board writer" because I wrote so well and straight, "like you have a ruler on the end of your nose," she'd say.

When I dare to be powerful—to use my strength in the service of my vision, then it becomes less and less important whether I am afraid.
—Audre Lorde

Truth is what works.
—William James

People wish to be poets more than they wish to write poetry, and that's a mistake. One should wish to celebrate more than one wishes to be celebrated.
—Lucille Clifton

The universe is made up of stories, not atoms.
—Muriel Rukeyser

Every day after class when I was helping out with the bulletin board or some other project she had me working on, she would tell me how great I was—what a great cheerleader I would make, how smart I was, what a leader I was in class, how good at athletics. At first I didn't believe a word she said. I thought she was stupid to think I had any of those skills, but eventually I began to believe her. As she fortified me with confidence, I found myself living up to her expectations. I *was* becoming a leader, I *was* the smartest kid in class, I *was* good at sports and the best blackboard writer in the class. On the day we held class elections, when Sister Helen counted the votes, every single vote but one (mine) was for me. I was elected class president, and I ran fourteen blocks all the way home to let my mom know that the kids really liked me. A metamorphosis had occurred, and a brand new butterfly was loose in the world.

It was that year I decided to become a nun when I grew up so I could do for other kids what Sister Helen Charles had done for me. It was like magic and I couldn't wait for six more years to pass so I could enter the convent and start making other kids feel as good as she made me feel. The only other career choice that had to go was circus acrobat. Even though I loved performing and doing dangerous tricks from the treetops for the neighborhood kids, I knew that my new calling was to be a nun and I never wavered in that knowing.

As it turns out, it wasn't the convent, but the part about service that rattled in my bones. What I felt to be my calling was not about poverty, chastity, and obedience but about nurturing others, feeding their spirits, helping them find their own beauty and strength. That, I can do anywhere.

In her article, Jean Houston reminds us that it is a privilege to be able to act on what one feels as a calling or destiny, as in many cultures children have no choice about what they will be when they grow up. For those of us in developed countries, she asserts that barriers to personal growth are caused more often by inertia than lack of choice. We end up spending our lives doing one boring job rather than do the work of discerning where our true passion lies and following that. And this happens not so much by intention as by default. She writes:

> We are educated, not for our time, but for some time around the mid-twenties. We need another training from somewhere else. We have to stop living as half-life versions of who and what we

Painting is a blind man's profession. He paints not what he sees, but what he feels, what he tells himself about what he has seen.
—*Pablo Picasso*

The lesson that one's experience matters, that it provides the best line to truth, is knowledge that we are born with, then taught to forget, and then learn anew.
—*Terri Apter*

Artistic growth is more than it is anything else, a refining of the sense of truthfulness. The stupid believe that to be truthful is easy; only the artist, the great artist, knows how difficult it is.
—*Willa Cather*

really are. If we are to become in reality stewards of the Earth, cocreators in the great enterprise of an expanding reality, if we are to respond adequately to who and what is calling us, then we must democratize greatness and do remedial work in essence.

Even though essence is a concept that cannot be adequately described, we each know when it happens if we have somehow tapped into it. There is a certain charge to that moment, a certain lightness to the energy around our body. A tingly feeling might race through us, or we might find tears of joy in our eyes or a trembling in our bones. We are never tired, never sluggish, and our bodies feel energized by an uncanny and unusual force.

Whenever I touch my essence, I have the strongest feeling that I am doing just what I came to this earth to do. I don't often feel it in my physical body like that, but when I do, I am suffused with joy. For me, it happens when I am serving people, in the simplest of ways—if I am making tea for a sick friend or carrying a grocery bag for an older woman.

This feeling also occurs when I am in a large group of women. I have never been able to figure this out, but there is a certain energy released that seems to enter into me and lift me up onto some higher emotional level. It happens whenever I return to the Motherhouse for a visit and always at the International Women's Writing Guild Conference, where 450 women gather for a week to learn and share and renew their creative energy. During that week, I feel tapped into my essence in an extraordinary way. It feels as though I am hooked up to some source of pure energy, pure joy and creativity.

I have always been so mystified by this phenomenon that I was delighted to find Houston's account of just such an experience:

When we touch into essence, latent actions and skills suddenly jump into life. The reason for this explosion of energy and possibilities is that essence has many more capacities than does the local self—because the local self is carved out of the conditions of day-to-day existence. . . . When you begin to activate these capacities of essence, they gather information from beyond

---

It's very difficult to find in the outside world something that matches what the system inside you is yearning for.
—*Joseph Campbell*

If our life lacks a constant magic, it is because we choose to observe our acts and lose ourselves in consideration of their imagined form instead of being compelled by their force.
—*Antonin Artaud*

Music comes first from my heart, and then goes upstairs to my head where I check it out.
—*Roberta Flack*

the physical senses. The extraordinary capacities linked to essence access—what should we say?—news from the universe.

Houston proposes that, in a state of essence, because all systems and senses are on *go*, we know with such a simultaneity of knowing that we can be said to have grasped the whole of anything. "Such knowing brings a clarity, a certainty, a precision that seldom comes from reasoning, intuition, or insight," she writes. "The deepest values, purposes, and patterns for life, the richest potential coding for existence, the source level for creative, innovative action and ideas become known to us through essence."

Creativity is not something that has to be worked at, but something that is released automatically when we are on the right path. It is a natural part of us, a force waiting to be released, inherent in each and every one of us. If we feel blocked in our creativity, perhaps we should take another look at what we've made of our life and see how close it comes to reflecting the real essence of who we are.

It's frightening to think of reinventing our lives, but consider the vast possibilities that may open up once you've committed to a life that's in line with your true calling. Why not start from scratch and imagine what you would choose to do if you had it to do all over again?

You could start with the lottery conversation. What would you do if you won the lottery? This is a good way of getting at the dream inside that is stifled by external constraints. Last year I asked my partner, Annie, this question. She responded immediately, "I'd go to law school." Never in all the years I have known her did she once mention law school, and now at the thought of not having to worry about money, it came up like her big dream in life.

My response was to figure out how we could make that dream a reality, so we began our research. We narrowed it down to the states we would be happy to live in and sent away for catalogs from several universities. Annie set up appointments with lawyers in the field of healthcare and law and put all her questions out on the table. She also took a law class at the local university to see if it felt like a good fit. The process took more than a year, and by the end of our research she had figured out that it wasn't a law degree but a Ph.D. in biomedical ethics that would enable her to do the work she wants to do in the world. Now at

If a child is to keep alive his inborn sense of wonder without any such gift from the fairies, he needs the companionship of at least one adult to share it, rediscovering with him the joy, excitement and mystery of the world we live in.
—Rachel Carson

I can always be distracted by love, but eventually I get horny for my creativity.
—Gilda Radner

the ages of forty-seven and forty-eight, we are uprooting our lives and heading to California on a path that's in alignment with her dream in life.

Who knows where we'd be if the lottery question hadn't come up, but I imagine we'd be hunkering down for winter in the snowy Northeast. It's a vital time for us, fertile, full of inquiry and a sense of quest. And even though a certain level of fear and anxiety comes along with an unknown of such dimension, the sense of being on the right track is far more compelling.

Following one's dream doesn't always mean pulling up roots and relocating. It could happen with no geographic change at all. The point is to ask ourselves and our partners the essential questions so that we don't get burrowed into a lifestyle that is comfortable but far from the mark.

To live creatively is to live from the soul, to shape our circumstances out of our deepest desires instead of conforming our dreams to the circumstances in which we find ourselves. Once we experience the joy and power of creating our own lives, we find that creating in other arenas comes naturally, an outflow of the abundant energy that comes with being true to our essence.

As soon as knowledge is allowed to be intuitive and sensory in origin and its intellectual roots are seen to be in various kinds of perception, everyone is allowed in. It then becomes literally true that everyone is an artist.
—Harold Taylor

Meditations and Actions

1. Rent the video *Phenomenon* and notice what changes for the character when he begins to access his deeper potential. What might change for you if you had access to these powers? What would you do with them? How would you like to be of use?

2. Remember a time in your childhood when you felt a strong calling to something, as if it were your destiny. Write about it in your notebook or discuss it with a friend. Be particular about the details: What were you doing that brought it on? How did you respond to this feeling? Did it happen often? Are you doing anything now that brings back those feelings? What activities do you now engage in that bring you joy? Is there any connec-

tion between these activities and the feelings you had as a child about your destiny? Has something external kept you from actualizing the dreams in your life? If you had your life to do over, what would you do differently? Why not do it?

3. Take a calendar and set aside one week as a "Week of Dreams." Imagine that money is no issue and fill in each day with activities that bring you a feeling of well-being. What would you be doing with your life if you were totally responsible for creating it? Who or what *is* responsible for what your life looks like?

4. Light a candle and put on some soothing music. In your notebook, write a letter to your Muse. Explain that you want to get in touch with the essence of who you are. Tell her everything you know about your essence and everything you want to know but are unsure about. Tell her when you have felt most in touch with it, and what happens when you drift away. Ask her to help you with this process and then begin to write, paying no attention to the words as they come. Write as fast as you can, letting the thoughts flow freely onto the page. Do not stop to think or edit or erase. Keep writing until the song you are listening to comes to an end, then read what your Muse has written on the subject of your essence. (The power of this exercise often seems magnified in a group setting, with three or more people calling on help from their inner spirits. You might want to consider forming a small group and doing some common writing on a weekly basis.)

5. If possible, talk to someone who knew you as a child. Ask that person what they remember about you, what characteristics stand out as memorable from your childhood years. Compare those memories with your contemporary self and notice what has changed the most since you were young. What do you think contributed to these changes?

6. Think of the friends in your life whom you consider to be creative. What do they do? What makes them happy? In what ways are they different from the friends you don't consider creative? Where do you fall on the creativity continuum? What would

you have to do to think of yourself as more creative? Where did that standard come from?

Music Suggestions

Benedictine Monks of Santo Domingo de Silos, *Chant* (Angel Records)
Ottmar Liebert and Luna Negra, *Soro Para Ti* (Higher Octave Music)
Suzanne Ciani, *History of My Heart* (Private Music)
Best of Rachmaninoff (Philips)
Highlights from Julian Bream (BMG Classics)
Carlos Nakai, *Desert Dance* (Canyon Records)
Narada Decade—The Anniversary Collection (Narada)

Eliminate Your Enemies

A few years ago I was visiting my friend Ruby Lee in southern Kentucky. When Sunday morning rolled around, she hauled me off with her to the Baptist Church. While we were waiting for the service to begin, Ruby Lee leaned over and, in a hushed voice, told me to check out the woman at the organ. "She's the minister's wife," she whispered, "but he's having an affair with that blond woman in the second row of the choir. His wife is so mad she's spitting nails and she won't even look at him during the service anymore."

Before I could respond, the minister appeared and the organist started hammering out the processional hymn, her face starched into a sour expression, her eyes on the music and nowhere else. The blond in the choir was radiant, singing out jubilantly and smiling sweetly as the minister took his place on the altar. Ruby Lee leaned over again. "The whole congregation knows and a whole big mess is brewing—and just look at him. Why, who in her right mind would fall for him anyway?"

There were a few prayers said, but my mind was occupied with this triangular drama. I kept watching the organist, who was flipping madly through a folder of song sheets. She nibbled constantly at her bottom lip and avoided eye contact with anyone in the church. The new love object was sitting primly in her pew, gazing lovingly at the balding, overweight minister.

He walked as if he owned the world, his shiny robe rustling as he swaggered to the pulpit from center stage. "Brothers and sisters," he bellowed as he raised his arms in a welcoming gesture to the crowd, "today we're here to speak of our enemies, and to follow the Lord's call to love those enemies."

I didn't know who or what he thought the enemy was, but he said the word with such vehemence it gave me a fright. I looked over at Ruby Lee to see what she made of this, but she was calm as a cucumber, nodding her head in zealous approval. Ruby Lee was seventy-two years old. She

If the building of the bridge does not enrich the awareness of those who work on it, then the bridge ought not to be built.
—Frantz Fanon

It seems to me that the most integrative social power contained in words is liberated in performance. . . . For me, it is the activist and spoken element which follows on the contemplative act of composition which is most capable of vitalizing folk.
—Adrienne Rich

had spent every Sunday of her life in this church. For her, I guess, it was business as usual.

As he launched into his sermon, his deep voice rose to a fevered pitch and his robe billowed like a mainsail when he flailed his arms. The organist, by this time, was clipping her fingernails and the blond was sitting on the edge of her pew, rapt in devotion to the minister of her dreams. I tried to follow what he was saying, but every time he roared out the word enemy, I cowered a little deeper into the pew. After awhile, that was all I heard—enemy this, enemy that.

I don't know why I reacted so strongly to the word, but it's probably because I've spent my whole life trying not to have any. I wondered who he considered his enemies. Probably I'd be right in the mix, I thought, given who I am and what I stand for.

Then it occurred to me that I might be too naive and that maybe I *should* have an enemy or two. I worked on that for awhile and only a few names surfaced. Hitler came to mind right away, but he was already dead. People who bomb abortion clinics came to mind, and Klansmen, child abusers, gay-bashers, rapists—even my own—but I couldn't attach the title of enemy to any of them. Sick, yes. Dangerous, yes. Scary, yes—but not enemy. Not someone I would hurt or hate to talk to or hate in any way, except what they do. I hate how they hurt and polarize people and draw lines between themselves and others.

But to me, the enemy is that line that gets drawn, not the one who does the drawing. It's that severing that occurs when one of us forgets we are part of another.

When we came out of church I told Ruby Lee how I felt during the sermon, that I wanted to rush up to the pulpit and say, "No, don't try to love your enemies, try to eliminate them. Find a piece of yourself in that person you hate and get past that thing that keeps you separate." She threw her big yellow Oldsmobile into reverse and backed up into the chain link fence, "Girl, you sure got some strange ideas up there. C'mon, let's go git lunch."

We headed off to the local hospital for their Sunday buffet, but I couldn't get that minister off my mind. Maybe it's that preacher-wanna-be that lives somewhere deep inside me, I don't know, but for some reason I have terribly high expectations of people in positions of spiritual authority. From where I sat, he missed a big opportunity that

When you reach real ability you will be able to become one with the enemy. Entering his heart, you will see that he is not your enemy at all.
—*Tsuji*

It so happens that the work which is likely to be our most durable monument, and to convey some knowledge of us to the most remote posterity, is a work of bare utility; not a shrine, not a fortress, not a palace, but a bridge.
—*Harper's Weekly, 1883*

day, not to mention the havoc he was creating in who knows how many lives by having that affair.

Being a preacher is similar to being an artist, but with the added luxury of having a captive audience. It's a perfect opportunity to make a difference in people's lives, to add some new insight, to introduce a new concept, to create with words and gestures and music an event that really touches people and takes them deeper into their own thoughts and feelings.

With his words, that minister painted images that his congregation would carry with them throughout the week, the month, or even the duration of their lives. He took a reference from the Bible and developed a performance piece on the theme of enemy, and each of us perceived it through the filter of our own experience and expectations. Had there been critics in the audience, some would have panned him, others applauded.

On some level, we are all creators whether we intend to be or not. We constantly create environments which others enter, either to be nourished or negated. We create waves of energy that wash over our children, our coworkers, our lovers—waves that can lull and comfort or lash and damage. We create what our days and nights look like, what work we do, what beauty surrounds us. On a daily basis, we create the attitude we bring to life and choose whether the door to our heart is open or closed.

Like the preacher at the pulpit or the artist at her palette, we each create something for others to respond to, whether it is a sermon to reflect on, a painting to look at, or something as intangible as a safe space to be in. This is the privilege and the challenge of being alive.

The dividing line between good and evil passes, not between the other and me, but right down the middle of my forehead, between my left side and my right.
—Lanzo del Vasto

Instead of hating the people you think are war makers, hate the appetites and the disorder in your own soul, which are the cause of war.
—Thomas Merton

Creations, whether they are children, poems or organizations, take on a life of their own.
—Starhawk

Meditations and Actions

1. Imagine that you are asked to speak to a group of people on the subject of "The Enemy and What to Do with Him." What do you want to talk about?

2. Spend a day being mindful of the psychic space you create for

people around you. Pay attention to your body language, any negativity in your voice and words, the ways you move toward or away from people as they come into your path. Consider the people around whom you feel most comfortable. Give some thought to what they do with their body and energy to make you feel comfortable.

3. Go to your sacred space, light a candle, and give yourself thirty minutes to listen to *An English Ladymass* by Anonymous 4. While you're listening, consider whether there is anyone in your life you feel a need to reconcile with. Make a decision about what to do, perhaps to call or write a letter. Set aside time within the week to accomplish it.

4. Get the book *The Essential Rumi* (Harper and Row) with translations by Coleman Barks. Keep it at your bedside and read a poem every day before you get up and every night before you go to sleep.

5. Imagine that you are asked to give a speech to a writer's group in your community. They want you to develop your talk around a poem that has inspired you. What poem would you choose and what would you say about it?

6. Rent the video *Powder* (Caravan Pictures) and watch it with some children or teens. Talk about the movie and see if you're surprised by what they have to say.

The Workplace, the Wave, and the In-Between

A while ago, I met with two supervisors of a fairly large corporation to design a workshop that would help improve communications in the organization. It would be attended by twenty people in middle and upper management who gathered once a month for an hour to explore ways of working more effectively with each other. The meetings were planned and facilitated by different teams. On this day, it was up to the three of us to invent the next workshop. I came to the meeting buoyant with energy, delighted at the prospect of creating an event that could actually make a difference in how people communicated. Within twenty minutes I felt as though I was caught in a riptide.

My colleagues had arrived with cups full of caffeine and mindsets devoid of expectation. They were sure we were wasting our time on a worthless project, insisting that nothing we could do would ever change things. As they echoed each other's resounding doubt, the air grew heavy with negative energy. The space in my heart that was open for newness began to cave in with the weight of their words.

"This will never work. It never has in the past."

"These people are phonies. You can't trust half of them."

"What's the use? It's never going to go anywhere. Nothing will change around here."

"These meetings are always so boring. People would leave if they could get away with it."

The Mind Enemy was in our midst. My cocreators had given up before we'd even started, clinging to the past as if that was all we had to go on.

"Come on," I pleaded, "this is our chance to make it up any way we want. We have access to twenty people for one whole hour. There's so much we can *do* with that time. We can make magic happen." I knew we

We cannot wait for the world to turn, for times to change that we might change with them, for the revolution to come and carry us around in its new course. We are the future. We are the revolution.
—Beatrice Bruteau

Life shrinks or expands according to one's courage.
—Anaïs Nin

Those who lose dreaming are lost.
—Australian Aboriginal proverb

It is good to know the truth, but it is better to speak of palm trees.
—*Arabic proverb*

First you must find your trajectory, and then comes the social coordination.
—*Joseph Campbell*

I dream my painting and then I paint my dream.
—*Vincent van Gogh*

From my youth onwards, I have felt that all thought which thinks itself out to an issue ends in mysticism.
—*Albert Schweitzer*

could if we believed it, if we *each* believed it. But somehow, over the years, their faith in that kind of magic had turned to dust. And along with their faith went their vitality. They might as well have worn Do Not Resuscitate signs around their necks.

For the next hour, I tried to chip away at the walls they had built, tried to help them see the opportunity that existed for us to create a workshop that would really contribute to people, tried to have them see themselves and each other more clearly and compassionately; but their disillusion overpowered my attempts. No way, they said, no way.

We managed to create an agenda for the meeting, but we didn't create magic, nor anything unique and original. We didn't spend our time inventing something brilliant, for that involves risk and trust, and would have been possible only if each of us had come to the table with willingness in our hearts. Instead, while one fought for the light, another pointed to the darkness, and it was darkness that prevailed.

On the drive home from work that day, I listened to a tape of a Tibetan monk speaking about the imminence of death and the importance of seizing the opportunity of our lives while we have the chance. I thought of those two supervisors and wondered what it must be like to cling so steadfastly to hopelessness, to really believe that we are powerless beings, subject to the force of whatever wave we find ourselves in.

I thought of a recurring nightmare I've had since I was a child and how it has changed over the years as I have changed. The first few times I had the dream (or the dream had me, as some suggest), I would be standing on shore with my family around and my back to the ocean. Someone would scream at me to turn around and, as I'd turn, I'd see a huge tidal wave about to crash down on all of us.

Over time, the family disappeared from the scene, and I was alone facing the tidal wave. Then later, as I dreamed it, I would be high up on a cliff, close enough to be frightened by the wave's immensity, but far enough not to be caught when it crashed to the shore.

The last two times I experienced this dream, I was in the water when I saw the wave coming. At first, I was terrified as always. The wave was still ominous—roaring, tall as a skyscraper, dark, foreboding, and a sign, it seemed, of imminent death. In the first of these two dreams, I was under a wharf with huge wooden pilings. When the wave hit, I clung to a piling with so much strength that I pulled it out of the earth. It came out like a tree, roots and all, and I straddled it and rode it safely to shore.

At the last dreaming, I was in the water again, only there was nothing nearby but a few dolphins. When I looked toward the horizon and saw the wave coming, I was no longer horrified. I waited for it, waited to surf it. I watched its approach with a careful eye, studying its pace as it rumbled toward me. When I saw its cresting ridge towering above my head, I stretched my body taut and long and kicked into the curl, swimming with all my might. The wave and I became one, frolicking as we rolled and thundered, dolphins leaping at our side.

I don't know what this dream means in relation to that meeting, but I think it has something to do with believing in change, with knowing that things progress on their own, with or without our influence, but that the energy and posture we bring to any situation have a great deal to do with how it unfolds. William James wrote that the "greatest revolution in our generation is that human beings, by changing the inner attitudes of their minds, can change the outer aspects of their lives."

This is not to be interpreted as some New Age antidote to social injustice. A mother cannot provide food for a hungry child by visualizing bread, any more than a battered woman can change her abuser's behavior by changing her inner attitude. These injustices need to be confronted in very real terms with well thought-out strategies and public policies.

What James is suggesting is that the contours of our outer lives are shaped significantly by our inner reality. My relationship with the tidal wave changed over the years in accordance with changes that occurred within me. When I perceived the life force as something outside myself, something huge and powerful over which I had no control, it terrified me. It had the power to destroy me, and all I could do was run away from it.

As I grew older and began to perceive the life force as something that emanated from within me, I no longer needed to fear. I could engage with it, use it, enjoy it. And since it was no longer outside me, but within me, I did not need to control or run from it. I needed merely to try to understand it.

What turned the tide in that dream and, in fact, in the whole of my life, was a change in my belief regarding my own inner power. I know that I am touched by another's spirit, and I know that others are touched by mine. I know that when negative forces pull me, my capacity to hurt is

Two boys arrived yesterday with a pebble they said was the head of a dog until I pointed out that it was really a typewriter.
—Pablo Picasso

We must travel in the direction of our fear.
—John Berryman

The only way to love a person is not, as the stereotyped Christian notion is, to coddle them and bring them soup when they are sick, but by listening to them and seeing and believing in the god, in the poet, in them. For by doing this, you keep the god and poet alive and make it flourish.
—Brenda Euland

as powerful as my capacity to heal when I am pulled by the light. I know that I am free to choose which force to tie my reins to, as they both flow through me every moment Whatever I choose colors my world, both inner and outer.

There is no force outside me dictating my response to life. There is no reason for me to think this is the way it will always be or to believe that I have no power. Every moment brings a chance to choose—to act or be acted upon, to laugh or to cry, to open my arms or turn my back.

I did not for a minute think that when I sat with those two supervisors we would design a workshop that would change the organization. One does not change corporate culture by one workshop alone. We make change by believing in our power, by acting out of our inner force, and by acknowledging the power in the person at our side. It happens one by one, first in ourselves, then in another and another and another.

This is the magic I wanted to make happen. I wanted the three of us to be greater than we each were alone, to create a workshop that would help our colleagues and ourselves move a few steps forward. And we could have, I think, if my colleagues had believed it possible.

But maybe when they listened, it was the roar they heard. *That wave, oh no, coming again. . . .*

If you ask me what I came to do in this world, I, an artist, will answer you: I am here to live out loud.
—*Emile Zola*

The way to have good ideas is to have a lot of ideas and throw away the bad ones.
—*Linus Pauling*

Meditations and Actions

1. Start noticing any negativity you project. Keep a small notebook with you and when you realize that you've spoken negatively about someone or something, write it down. If someone asks what you are doing, be open and explain that you are trying to become aware of your display of energy. It's simply awareness we're after here.

2. When you're in a conversation with someone who is talking about something they don't like, see if you can reframe it so they focus on what it is they *want*. Do this with yourself as well.

3. Make a list in your notebook entitled "What Is Wrong with My Life." Write down everything that's wrong. Next to each entry, write down what would have to happen to turn that wrong into a right. Continue to do whatever you want.

4. Come to terms with the fact that you are creating your life. You have twenty-four hours a day to play with. How are you using that time? Is there anything you'd like to change? What can you do to have your days feel more like your idea than someone else's?

5. If you are in a conversation that evokes negative feelings, admit those feelings to the person you are speaking with and see what can be done to resolve them. Address whatever negativity you feel at the time so you don't have to carry that energy throughout your day.

Jewels in Our Midst

When I was in my twenties, I trekked around Europe for a couple months with two friends. My friend Bonnie brought her guitar everywhere and we'd often rip it out on a street corner and entertain the crowds with tunes by all the popular folksingers of the decade. We had quite a repertoire. By the time we ran through it, her guitar case would be loaded with francs, marks, or shillings.

Our other friend, Margaret, usually stood on the sidelines, occasionally singing, but most often playing yin to our yang, receiving whatever we sent out on the air waves. Every musical group needs an audience, and Margaret always played that part well. She clapped along, tapping out the beat in her hiking boots, listening every bit as actively as we were singing.

I don't remember that either of us ever asked Margaret if she wanted to sing with us. Bonnie and I had always been a duo and that was that, though Margaret was certainly welcome to sing along if she had wanted. She said she used to sing with her sisters when she was growing up, and she liked to sing, but she didn't seem to have the drive to perform like Bonnie and I did. There was nothing we loved more than a stage, nothing as exciting as an audience in front of us. But Margaret didn't need this. She was older and more secure than we. She didn't need applause from others to measure her worth.

We sang our way through several countries before we landed at a pub in Amsterdam that was owned by a former pianist of the renowned Dutch orchestra, the Concertgebouw. He was a strikingly handsome man, with a full head of white hair and a friendly face with a strong square jaw. We had read about his place in our bible, *Frommer's Europe on Five Dollars a Day*. The pianist was retired from the orchestra, but he had set up this pub with a grand piano and recordings of hundreds of concert pieces minus their piano parts. He accompanied these recorded tapes, playing live piano. The acoustics were remarkable, and the room, which

mitch had convinced sassafras that everything waz an art/so nothin in life cd be approached lightly/ creation waz inherent in everything anybody ever did right/that waz one of the mottos of the house.
—*Ntosake Shange*

If the only prayer you say in your whole life is "Thank You," that would suffice.
—*Meister Eckhart*

After silence, that which comes nearest to expressing the inexpressible is music.
—*Aldous Huxley*

was big enough to accommodate only ten to twelve tables, actually sounded like a concert hall when he played.

We ordered some aquavit from the bartender and sat at a table near to the piano. It was a weeknight and fairly slow, so the owner came over and spent some time talking with us. At the end of the conversation, Margaret asked him if he had the music to a certain song. He thought he did and walked to his stacks of tapes and sheet music to see if he could find it.

A few minutes later he motioned Margaret over to the piano. Bonnie and I were so busy downing our aquavits, ordering Bloody Marys, and searching through our guide book for new hot spots that we hadn't even noticed she was gone. It wasn't until we *heard* Margaret that we even looked up from our book and realized what was going on.

Margaret, in a voice as sweet and powerful as Maria Callas', was singing "Mon Coeur S'ouvre a Ta Voix" from Saint-Saëns' opera, *Samson and Delilah.* There she was, standing close to the piano, eyes closed, hands folded at her waist, her face turned up in a sweet smile as the most unbearably beautiful notes left her lips. I had never heard this kind of passion in a song before; never been exposed to that blend of music and emotion, that ability to translate the power of love into sounds so perfectly pitched, so rich in feeling that they pulled the tears right out of my eyes.

And this passion was coming from our Margaret—Margaret, who rarely sang but always listened; Margaret, my friend of all those years, who had this gift I never knew of, never asked about, never sought to uncover. I cried through the whole aria, laid my head in my arms and sobbed—half at the sheer beauty of the music, half in shame and embarrassment that I had never noticed the jewel in our midst.

I've always been ridiculously critical of myself. Part of the reason I have all this unfinished work kicking around is because I thought it wasn't good enough. I'm much freer now, a little bit easier on myself. I have the attitude that not everything has to be perfect. If it expresses some idea or truth, or some reality of what you believe, and if you can put it together in a way that doesn't embarrass you, then you should put it out.
—Steve Brown

As a writer you are about the freest person that ever was. Your freedom is what you bought with your solitude, your loneliness.
—Ursula LeGuin

Meditations and Actions

1. Get a tape or CD of *Sampson and Delilah* out of the library (Ultimate Opera, Collection 2, Warner Classics Unlimited). Go to your sacred space, light a candle, and play the aria "Mon Coeur S'ouvre a Ta Voix." See what happens.

2. Imagine that each of your close friends has a secret talent they have never been encouraged to express. See if you can discern what this gift is. Look for signs, such as what makes them happy and when are they most invigorated. Take some time to talk to them about this gift and encourage them in their creative expression.

3. Honor yourself with a gift of the audio cassette version of Bill Moyers' PBS Series, *The Language of Life—A Festival of Poets.* Consider it an investment in your creative future. (You can probably find it in a good library, but it is something you will want to keep.) Listen to some of it every day until you have heard every tape.

4. Pay attention to how you listen to people and notice if you are more concerned with expressing yourself than with truly communicating. Try this experiment: when you are in a conversation with someone, make a concerted effort to respond to what they are saying by asking questions rather than making statements of your own. Try to have one complete conversation where your only responsibility is to listen thoroughly and ask engaging questions. Was this difficult? Why? Did the person you were listening to seem to have a good time? Wouldn't you?

There are hundreds of ways to kneel and kiss the ground.
—*Rumi*

An old woman is never old when it comes to the dance she knows.
—*Ibo proverb*

*If I read a book and it makes my whole body so cold no fire can ever warm me, I know **that** is poetry. If I feel physically as if the top of my head were taken off, I know **that** is poetry. These are the only ways I know it. Is there any other way?*
—*Emily Dickinson*

Art does not reproduce the visible; rather it makes it visible.
—*Paul Klee*

One day Chao-Chou fell down in the snow and called out, "Help me up! Help me up!" A monk came and lay down beside him. Chao-Chou got up and went away.

Zen koan

Pass the Stardust, Please

I sit at a large round table surrounded by people who have gathered to share stories of their creative work and process. They have come from all sorts of places and work in all genres of art. They are music makers, storytellers, dancers, sculptors, poets, photographers, weavers, painters, printmakers, writers, creators of all things beautiful. They have committed their lives to what they love, and they use media to express who they are and what they see and feel.

One by one, they take their turns and speak about their work, about what it means to them to be living creative lives. Some speak of the freedom, the great release of tension and passion; some speak of the fear of feeling inadequate and how they struggle to overcome it; others speak of the Muse, the inner voice that calls them to the work; and some speak of creating as a sacred activity, one that involves spirit as much as flesh.

As my turn approaches to talk about my work, I start to worry. I feel unworthy of this time and attention, inferior to the others, a sparrow to their eagleness. Over the years, I have written deeply, but my words now seem shallow and trite. I have filled drawers with stories, photographs, songs, and poems created from nothing but the experience of my life, and a voice from somewhere calls them useless. I do not know why this doubt arises, but I am gripped by its power and unable to speak.

A woman at my side senses my anxiety. She draws near to touch my

The fundamental delusion of humanity is to suppose that I am here and you are out there.
—Yasutani Roshi

The future depends entirely on what each of us does every day.
—Gloria Steinem

hand. In a soft, gentle voice she says to the group, "Pass the stardust, please—my sister is forgetting." A small bowl of twinkling, iridescent stardust is passed to her and she dips in her fingertips to gather some. Leaning toward me, she sprinkles the stardust over my head and says in a whisper, "This will help you remember all you have created and all that it is worth."

As the sparkling stardust settles, I feel a certain lightness, and a wave of comfort passes over me. I start to remember that I was born to create, that all my life I have manifested beauty from the inside out. I remember that I have made and given to the world gifts that only I could have made and given from the treasures I have found on the paths that I have traveled. I remember that this is true for each of us, and that I am surrounded by creators longing to create and pass on the beauty they've found along the way. And I remember too that the future as well is ours to create, in consort with each other and the Great Creator.

My focus returns to the circle of artists and I begin: "I am an artist, creating with you . . ."

While this was just a dream, it was one that had enough energy to poke its way into consciousness and bring me courage in the process. Perhaps there are artists out there who never forget, creators who know in their bones every minute of the day what they are here to do and why they are doing it. Perhaps there is a state of awareness one reaches where doubt does not enter and fear can find no home. But for now, when I find myself forgetting, I am grateful for those in my life who help me remember; grateful for those who circle around me, tell me their stories, and ask to hear mine. It is this circle of sharing that keeps the work flowing, not only through me but out of me into the world.

Few of us can keep our faith if we work in a vacuum or void. None of us can convey our stories, pass on what we are here to pass on if we do not create for ourselves a circle of listeners. As crucial as it is to reach within and find the words we need to speak, it is equally crucial to extend ourselves outward, to believe ourselves into that next act of sharing our work.

It is time for us to trust in what we have to say, to bring it up out of our depths, let it find its way, and love whatever surfaces. It is time to release the stories, free the images, give shape to the clay of our lives and know the gift we bring this way is to the world.

God made everything out of nothing, but the nothingness shows through.
—*Paul Valery*

A true believer begins with herself.
—*Berber proverb*

One of the very worst, self-murdering lies that people tell themselves is that they are no good and have no gift and nothing important to say.
—*Brenda Euland*

All language is a longing for home.
—*Rumi*

Remember this: your creations are the mirror in which the rest of us find ourselves. Your stories and poems and paintings contain the seeds we need to grow our own. Your work is the music our lives can dance to, the light our eyes can see by. As you look to the writers, the poets, the musicians, and the storytellers for whatever truths they have to offer, we look to you for the same. We need each other. We need this light that shines from your deep down, so do not hide it. Do not be afraid. Let it shine. Breathe it out. Give it life. And if you falter, if you forget the value of your work, think of us at your side, stardust in hand.

Meditations and Actions

1. Go into your sacred space and light a candle. Play "Song for the World" from Paul Winter's *Wolf Eyes* (Living Music Records). Feel the presence of every artist in the world and know they are on your side. See them reaching out for you, gathering you into the circle, and see yourself entering, celebrating the part you play in adding beauty to the world. Be joyful and give thanks for this amazing gift.

2. Create a commitment ceremony for you and your Muse. Whether you do this alone or with other artists, plan an event that is as celebratory as it is sacramental. Buy flowers, bring balloons, choose the perfect music, burn incense, light candles, write vows, and speak them loudly and with total commitment. If you can, make time for a honeymoon and see what happens.

3. Join a national organization of artists who work in your medium. Make plans to attend its annual conference. These organizations are listed in trade magazines, or you may inquire at your local university or library. (For writers, I suggest the International Women's Writing Guild, Box 810 Gracie Station, New York, NY 10028.)

4. Take an art class for the fun of it at your local community college. If you're a writer, try drawing or pottery. If you're a painter, try

In order to write a poem, place yourself in contemplative expectation before a blank piece of paper, put your hand on the paper and your hand will write your way to the poem.
—Carolyn Forche

Opportunities are like pole beans. You have to keep picking them so more can grow.
—Hope Wallis

Love is this—that two solitudes border, protect, and salute one another.
—Rainer Maria Rilke

Effort is the problem, not the solution.
—Deepak Chopra

a creative writing class. Experiment with another art form and see how its sharpens your creative edge.

It is a risk to connect. But the artist—the ones the Creator shows—does so with the understanding that connection itself is simply the expression of her or his being, and that not to at least make the effort is to die.

—Alice Walker

5. Organize an *On Your Own Time* exhibition at your workplace. Send a memo around for anyone who does creative work to prepare something to be exhibited at the worksite or in your local gallery, library, or bank. It will be good PR for your employer and will provide you with an opportunity to see who is creating what in your working environment.

6. Find a way to package your work for sharing. If you write stories or poems or songs, make a cassette tape of them and pass them out to friends and family. If you paint or draw or make photographs, create a booklet of your work and make enough copies to hand out. If you are a dancer or musician, organize an evening of entertainment with a few other colleagues at your local coffeehouse or church basement. Tie it into an event like International Women's Day, Mother's Day, Black History Month, Gay Pride Month, etc. and celebrate your gifts while raising consciousness at the same time.

7. Listen to the poem "Cry" by Jimmy Santiago Baca on the cassette tape series from Bill Moyers' PBS Special *Celebration of Life— A Festival of Poets.* Have your notebook open, and when it is done, make a list of all the reasons you are now crying. (If you are not crying, listen to it again and give yourself permission to open up. Crying is so healing.) When you review your list, choose something from it that you will use as an impetus for a creative work. See what happens when you begin to transform a life experience into a work of art.

PART THREE

Passing the Stardust

Because we often find encouragement in each other's
stories, this section includes writings from artists
who share what they have encountered on their own
creative journeys. Each of them has braved the
darkness while heading toward the light. Each has struggled against fear,
doubt, isolation, and cultural constraints; each has managed to make
their way as an artist in the world.

These are stories of possibility and stories of breaking out, breaking
into, breaking through. They are here as wind for your sails, candles to
your dark, the voices of your sisters and brothers calling you forth.

Poem of Sustenance

This is the poem that stands
in the moonlight singing,
that rises from sleep
because in darkness stars
are seen, because in darkness
you see what you will
and in darkness you dream.

And when fear washes
you away and the moon
is a cold light vanishing,
this is the poem that swims
among the coral casting
its net for the small
yellow fish or the stars.

Sheila Bender

About seven years ago, I began studying the Enneagram, *An Ancient System for Understanding Yourself and Others in Your Life*, as Helen Palmer subtitles her groundbreaking book of 1988, *The Enneagram*. I found her book in a Berkeley bookstore the year I was living there with my husband, who had temporarily transferred companies. When we returned to our home in Seattle, I discovered that Jesuits were teaching courses in the Enneagram through Seattle University. I went to several of the intensives, and I learned quite a lot about the system, myself, my spirituality, and how writing was a part of my spirituality.

Taught in oral tradition by the secret mystery school of the Sarmouni Brotherhood to Russian spiritualist Gurdjieff and Chilean spiritualist Ichazo, who then both taught others, the Enneagram of personality goes beyond ordinary life. It discusses, in the words of California scholar Charles Tart, "the existential and spiritual virtues that could be developed if we recaptured the essential life energy that was going into pathological defenses against our real nature."

I had discovered for myself, learning to write poetry and studying with master poets as I approached thirty, that writing was my ticket to true authenticity. It was my way of knowing the world and my relationship to both it and the people I knew in it. Discovering the truths in my finished poems was both frightening and life enhancing. I began to perceive things and to say them after a lifetime of trying not to see or say too much. I had grown up in a postwar first-generation family where too much truth would upset the apple cart, forcing family members to look at the guilt they used as both motivator and inhibitor and to examine their careless and damaging intrusions into other family members' lives and psyches. I had never wanted to be an apple-cart upsetter, but growing up in the sixties and then writing in the eighties and nineties forced me to become one.

How can you write if you can't cry?
—Ring Lardner

By the time I discovered the Enneagram, I was forty, and had ten years of serious writing under my belt. In the Enneagram there are nine personality types, each with a chief feature that defines a particular method of attention similar to a neurosis or a defense that covers up a particular spiritual essence. I am point two, "the giver." Givers are raised with the understanding, Helen Palmer writes, that survival depends on the approval of others and that relationship is the most important area of existence. Givers alter themselves to meet other people's ideas of desirability. They work hard to help others and make themselves indispensable to the goals those others try to attain. Givers leave themselves little time to know themselves.

My mother was the first person I was hooked into helping. I am her oldest child, and I have read that the oldest is not quite separated from the ego of the parents. I could feel my mother's wishes as if they were palpable. I tried to keep myself from going against any of them. What a departure and "disturbance of the peace" (as Jack Gilbert calls poetry) my first real poem was, and how scared I felt to publish it when *Writer's Forum* in Colorado accepted it. How absolutely fitting it was as my first poem: it was a bulldozer, a plow, a machine for space clearing, an announcement.

Love is in supreme form, concentration.
—Patricia Sterne

My Mother Was Here Today

My mother was here today to try on the children
like garments in Bloomingdale's,
her praise stalking them for lines to flatter her,
while coins spilled from her fingers and perfume
crowded the heavy aroma of feelings.

Near the light my daughter crayons. I concentrate
by the window where silver dollar plants
and bear grass arrange my eyes.
"Emily," I ask my daughter, "what shall I
give to a fifty-year-old woman who makes
my eyes suddenly hard as diamonds?"

earrings, I am thinking.

"Mom," my daughter asks me, "what can I draw

for a twenty-nine-year-old woman
who knows I won't do a flower or a truck?"
We decide on a girl dangling from the moon.
Spreading arcs of yellow my daughter
works to make the sky larger.

The news this poem delivered was that I was going to embark on an adventure that would not meet with approval; I was hooked to the moon and therefore to creativity and would require a bigger horizon. And I had the support of my very young daughter who has continued to feel and know the truth.

Pride is the chief passion of a giver, and an evolving giver tries to convert that passion into the virtue of humility. I wrote my way, first in poetry and later in essays, from living through others by helping them and getting their approval, to understanding myself and my own needs. In fact, I understand now with help from the Enneagram studies and life experience that knowing my own needs allows me to extend just the right amount of giving to others so they are freer to be independent. I have begun to sort out when the demands of others are manipulative and when they are genuine, when I give in order to get, and when my giving is exactly what is required, no strings attached.

It does not surprise me that eighteen years after my first poem, I wrote this one for my daughter:

For My Daughter Who Has Gone To Study in Japan

Second full moon in one month tonight.
Through my skylight, I watch
it take its high place before I set binoculars
outside on a tripod and search its bright surface.

I see a navel on the moon as if it hung once
like a large fruit, white lines holding
its roundness like the ones on an orange under the peel.
I think of your arms growing tight around me
as your flight's boarding began and remember
to you the moon was always a brave soul,
lying on its back with its tiny little toes in the air,

Forget the doubts and fears that are creeping into your heart.
—Chinese fortune cookie

alone in the big blue sky and the funny moon didn't care.

I sang these words to you and never wondered
if the planet that gave birth to the moon
was as brave as her offspring, if vines and trees
mourned the dropping of their ready fruit.

As the first fall fog rolls in from Puget Sound, I walk
toward our front door crunching the fallen berries
of our mountain ash trees, almost believing
you will be inside, a girl once again under table light
folding origami paper into cranes, crossing cooking
skewers for a mobile to hang them from.

I sit awhile on the front porch staring into wet leaves,
listening for the quiet song earth sings, her belly
full of stems, her daughter far away and bright.

The moon is still an important symbol for me, linking me to my daughter and to creativity. The sky is larger in my life with her than it was in my life with my mother—I can let her go with all the joy and poignancy that act demands of me. She is not here to serve my needs, although my love for her serves my poetry.

It is perhaps no surprise, since I am a giver, that my Muse insists I be a teacher and facilitator of writing as well as a writer. In this area also I am learning when to help a student and when to hold back, when what I have to say will be helpful and when listening is the better idea. Most of all, I have realized that helping others to write well feels good and can be a contribution—I don't need it to buttress my feelings of self-worth. I teach because I can and it is needed. I write because I must. Writing is my proving ground, my darkroom developer; I use it to remember I am me unconditionally and that it is safe to be me. I am!

Humility is like standing naked in front of a mirror and being grateful for exactly what is reflected back, with no inclination to pridefully inflate one's feelings by imaging it as more than what it is, or to be deflated by not accepting what is really there.
—Helen Palmer

ℬio

Sheila Bender is a Seattle-area poet and writer. Her book of poems, *Love From the Coastal Route*, was published in 1991. She has written four books on writing: *Writing in a Convertible with the Top Down* (Warner Books, 1992 and reissued by Blue Heron Press in 1997); *Writing Personal Essays: How to Shape Your Life Experiences for the Page* (Writer's Digest Books, 1995); *The Writer's Journal* (Dell Publishing, 1997); and *Writing Personal Poetry* (Writer's Digest Books, 1998). Sheila has taught most recently as guest-writer-in-residence in Seattle University's undergraduate creative writing program.

Little Goddess Flying Down the Fall. 32″ x 56″. Acrylics and house paint on fabric.

Judith Ann Benedict

What got me started in art was looking at children's books when I was very young. From the beginning, I always loved books and the images in them. Books were a place of intimacy for me, as well as a way of exploring and traveling. My world wasn't very big, but through my books I could see the whole world, meet amazing characters, and experience lives quite different from my own. Because of this, my imaginary life was so rich, vivid, and exotic that many times it seemed more real than ordinary reality.

When I was little, I remember always looking at the other side of the illustration, the back side of the page, and wondering where did the picture go? For me, the pictures were like a movie, a magical image I could enter. I never knew if I was artistic or not. All I wanted was to be able to do what those artists did who drew those pictures. I wanted to create on a simple piece of paper everything that really wasn't there. None of what I saw in my picture books existed, but because those artists could draw and use colors so well, I could be transported into another whole world of time and history and place.

I wanted to be an artist and that's all there was to it. All the years that I have worked as a commercial artist, I've been haunted by the desire to write for children. In the back of my mind and the front of my heart, that desire kept me going; that's what I wanted to return to. And this year, now that I am nearly fifty, I'm going to have my first children's book published.

In my years as a commercial artist, the focus of my art was on communicating with others rather than on the power of creation itself. Now, I am less focused on what happens to others when they view my work as I am on what happens to me in the act of discovery and creation. Now the communication is from my nonverbal inner self to my conscious

Let yourself be silently drawn/By the stronger pull of what you really love.
—Rumi

The most exhausting thing you can do is to be unauthentic.
—Anne Morrow Lindbergh

outer self, and the bridge between these selves is the shared language of images. Creativity is no longer just a process that supports my external life, it also nourishes and feeds my essence.

A few years ago, during a creative dry spell, I had a profound dream. In it, I had no hands, just stumps. There came a day when I understood it was time to go get my new hands. I went to this place where a person came out with a pair of live hands and said, "OK, put your arms down here on this little pillow on this little table." They were happy and I was happy and it was very simple. They just pressed the hands to my stubs and said, "Oh, you've really got little wrists—these are the hands for you, but you've got really little wrists so we're just going to have to make them a little bigger." So they took a spray bottle, misted the stumps; the stumps swelled up just a bit and they said, "Perfect!" Then they stuck the hands on both ends, and I wiggled my fingers and they worked. This person said, "OK now, no gardening, no physical labor, no playing with your animals. You just rest and do simple things for twenty-four hours. After you do that they'll be perfect, they're on there forever, and you can do whatever you want."

This was one of those aware dreams in which I, the real Judith Ann, was consciously aware that I was dreaming this particular dream. I was so happy. I knew this dream had great significance for my art. I was getting my hands back! I was going to be able to work! But when I looked down at my hands in the dream, I was flooded with questions.

Whose hands are these? Who was the person in the dream who gave me these hands? Was it an angel spirit, my guardian, who gave me these hands? Did someone die in real life and leave me these hands? Was it a man, a woman, from long ago or from now? Whose hands did I receive? I couldn't tell if they were male or female hands.

I the dreamer and the consciously aware me had all these questions. As I looked down at my new hands, my conscious self felt kind of sad that the hands were not partially mine. The moment I had that wish, every other finger on my new hands turned back to fingers that I recognized as my own. And so every other finger on my new hands was my own finger and every other finger was from the mysterious hand of the "helper." Then I was totally pleased. I said, "This is perfect," and I woke up.

From that moment on, from that day on, every piece of art that I've

*Life breaks everyone . . .
but some grow stronger
at the broken part.*
—*Ernest Hemingway*

*What do you plan to
do with your one wild
and precious life?*
—*Mary Oliver*

envisioned I've been able to create, and everything I've made has come from an internal place deep inside of me. The synthesis was that there was this divine partnership between my hands, my working spirit and my abilities and that I had inherited, grown into, and *earned* my hands.

When I started the children's book I'm working on, I dreamt of the story for months, and all the characters and imagery came to me. I didn't have to strive for it, I just let them come to me. I have a little altar in my studio with a lake rock. On the rock is a Buddhist prayer: "May the god that is in all things be in me." I put my drawing hand on this stone and my left hand on my heart and say this prayer, asking that the art that comes from my hand comes from my heart and that the art is from the higher good and goes to the higher good. This is the only way I know how to work now, and in this way I feel the most genuine, the most real.

During the last year, two significant happenings have enriched my creative life. The first occurred one day when I opened a door, walked into a meditation room, and discovered the labyrinth. Immediately I recognized the ancient archetypal form, as I had been studying the goddess for years and completing a master's thesis on prepatriarchal imagery. On the floor before me was a forty-by-forty-foot canvas cloth, with the image of the labyrinth from Chartres Cathedral in France painted on it. When I saw it, I was overwhelmed on many levels and felt a profound recognition, deeper and older than my twentieth-century consciousness. For a moment, I was out of my time and place. I was sucked into the symbol and surrounded visually by it: I was in love with the image the moment I saw it and felt deeply at home, safe. At the same time, the conscious artist and scholar in me was identifying the image as a huge mandala with a flower center. Because of my studies, I knew what it was, what it stood for symbolically, and how it acted on the body, mind, and soul. However, experientially, it was a thrill!

Ordinarily we stand outside of art. Usually we cannot touch it or enter it except with our eyes. But here was this beautiful image, not up on a wall beyond my reach, but on the floor beckoning me to walk, to touch, to enter. As an artist, I had never walked on the "lines" of my drawings. I took off my shoes and socks and entered the labyrinth, following its winding path. I felt like Alice after she had eaten the mushroom that made her very small. Instead of me being big and the lines I draw being small, everything was reversed. The painted lines were so

When the artist has trained herself sufficiently, her hand takes on a life of its own, as she moves to create from her inner self; the balance between her conscious control, her heart, hands, and head renders her without willful ego, but now with only an expressive soul.

—Mary Hopkins

large that they made a path for me to travel on, to journey towards myself. The experience was wonderful, and when it was over I didn't want to leave the labyrinth's embrace and safeness. I committed then to creating a similar labyrinth, and over many months, this is coming to pass. I am now nearing completion on a forty-by-forty-foot canvas labyrinth for myself and others to journey on.

The other magical thing that has made such a difference in my life this year has been the mandala. I became reacquainted with this powerful form in a workshop with Judith Cornell, who was speaking at a conference I attended last year. Although I'd never read her book, *Mandala: Luminous Symbols of Healing,* everything she said touched my deeper knowing and was so familiar that hearing about the mandala for the first time was almost like hearing an echo. It was like a remembering of something I have always known.

I realized that when I work from inside of myself the work comes from the subconscious and speaks to my conscious mind. It comes from a place with which I can't readily have a dialogue. It comes up in image form and is manifested on a piece of paper in front of me, so my consciousness can see and acknowledge and actually communicate with what is essentially a message sent up from the soul. When I saw Judith Cornell, she was saying that in the mandala form your self is manifesting the essence of its nature, something it needs and wants to say that you need to know. The mandala is almost like food when it comes up, when it's visual and in front of you. Just as when a Catholic looks at the Sacred Heart or a Buddhist looks at a sacred relic or Tibetan sand painting, when you look at the spiritual manifestation of a mandala your eyes receive it back as food. It goes back into your body and the lines and the color and the shape have vibrations. It's like a prescription for what ails you. It may be a prescription to heal sadness or for joy, clarity, or forgiveness, but you trust whatever your soul self, your deep subconscious, sends up to you. Your soul is basically saying, "This is what you need to eat today." You look at the image the way people look at the face of a beloved. It's like taking your own communion.

For me, creating mandalas is like cooking good food for my soul. Sometimes it is a humble supper, other times I manifest a feast. Either way, it is visual food that comes up from my soul in a form that can be seen and used by my conscious self. Through the mandala drawings, my

Stop learning, start knowing.
—*Rumi*

When the question is well framed, the answer will come.
—*Jean Shinoda Bolen*

ancient timeless spirit is manifesting the essence of its nature right there in front of me on a simple piece of paper. And it is giving me something I need to have, feel, or know. I trust that whatever comes up from this deep kindness is the precise medicine or food needed at the moment. And in this presence, I feel the same wonder and awe I felt as a child, looking hard and deep into my picture books. Another little piece of the mystery is revealed and I see myself—face to face. Like a circle completing itself, it rises up out of me, through my hands onto the paper, to be absorbed by my eyes and back down into my heart.

Bio

Judith Ann Benedict lives in upstate New York by the shores of Lake Ontario. She shares her country home with her husband, Mark, along with a menagerie of ducks, cats, and the world's most beautiful dog. An avid gardener and animal lover, her fascination with the natural world can be seen in her work. Trees are her favorite neighbors and she marks her calendar with the blooming of the first snowdrops, the return of the hummingbird "scout," and the full moons.

Jude has been drawing all her life, the last twenty-nine years of them professionally. An award-winning illustrator, designer, and artisan, her images can be found all over the world, in books and magazines, on posters and cards, printed on fabric, painted on wood, and etched in stone. She has taught art and design in college for many years and shared her expertise with children as well as adults through many workshops on creativity, illustration, and the business of art. Her first children's picture book, *When Dawn Stole the Dark* written by Donna Joerg, was published in 1997 by Cadence Press.

God's Teeth

God's teeth
are the color of berries.
From far off they could be anybody's
teeth, but close up you see
when she laughs
that her mouth is on fire!

What is it
she's after, crouching and grinning there
in the shadows, her teeth
so convincing
you cannot look away? You count
in secret:

in spite of her age they are all there,
those grinders and rippers, rooted
in her gums like redwoods,
the kind you lean against grinning,
to show the friends back home you've got what it takes
to set the world
on fire.

Only this time the light snaps
shut. You're a red
berry. You are lodged
between her teeth. And all night
that rough
tongue will search you out, all night
she will pull and suck on the straws of you,
till the skin cracks,
and the sap turns sweet,

and you run at last
into the mouth of God
like wine.

Karen Elias

A student once jokingly told me, after I'd shared some of the details of my life in a course I was teaching on autobiography, that I have "taken the scenic route." She was right. Raised to be a good daughter in the conservative fifties, trained to imagine my life as a neatly wrapped package, I have, from that perspective, done it all wrong. Committed to having children *and* a career, it took me years, for instance, to finish the coursework for my academic degrees because I was at the same time raising three boys. From another perspective, though, it occurs to me that perhaps I've attempted to bring together, in the space of one life, ways of knowing that have too often been split apart. Insisting stubbornly on a kind of imagined wholeness, I have sometimes carried my possibilities like a rucksack full of feisty, bickering animals. How to make sense of it all. I guess if we're talking about ways of knowing, the place to start is here, with school.

I have been in school almost all my life. From the beginning, I was rewarded for doing well in school. And from the beginning, I loved being there. I loved the almost visceral pleasure I would get from exploring the new territory I found in books. In first grade, something unexpected happened to me. it was probably the beginning of winter. I had been sent to school wearing a snowsuit that required a great deal of snapping and zipping. We were about to go outside for gym, and I was struggling in the cloakroom with my unwieldy snowsuit. When I finally walked out, ready to join the class, the room was empty. I remember seeing a room I had recently loved become in that moment a foreign land, requiring sudden courage to navigate. I walked to the door. It was locked. Still mostly undaunted, I lifted the long pole with its hooked end from its narrow recess by the windows, and, like the trapeze artists I had seen in the circus, balanced it just right until it fit the proper notch. I pulled, and the window opened. I dragged the teacher's chair over to the window and

Inanna asked: "What is this?" She was told: "Quiet, Inanna, the ways of the underworld are perfect. They may not be questioned."
—*Inanna, Queen of Heaven and Earth, Diane Wolkstein and Samuel Noah Kramer*

Let the beauty we love/ Be what we do.
—*Rumi*

leaned out, yelling to her that I was still there, that I needed her to come back: Miss Morse, Miss Morse! But she was out of hearing. I remember seeing her straight back and the line of children behind her: the habitual midmorning trip to the playground. After that, I remember only a voice coming from my mouth that belonged to someone I did not recognize. This was someone who screamed and cried and banged so loudly on the walls that the teacher in the next room—from all I've been able to gather—got the master key from the principal's office and let me out. I became myself once again. Silently, I joined the class on the playground, grateful that no one had noticed my absence. When we got back to the classroom, Miss Morse took one look at the disarray—her chair, a potted plant, the window pole all out of place—and asked who was responsible for the mess her classroom had become? I remember my face flaming with sudden fire, remember slithering down into my seat with the new knowledge that I had been wrong, *I* was wrong, *I* was the bad girl.

At my son's wedding last year, my mother gave me a packet of old clippings and photographs, things she had been saving for me for years, things that she now wanted me to have. In the packet was a photograph of my first-grade class. There at the blackboard is Henry Hamburger, the math genius, and there sitting at their first-grade desks are Barbara Kirkham and Leslie Torkelson and Virginia Wulf, my best friend who would die of leukemia in the fifth grade. There is Alan Pease at the easel, and behind him, below the clock, are paintings we have done of butterflies. I recall the morning this picture was taken. My mother, knowing the photographer will be there that day, has brushed my hair with extra care and has sent me to school with roses from her garden. In the picture I stand at the back of the room next to the teacher, arranging these roses, a flowery, beatific smile on my face. For a long time after getting this picture from my mother my impulse was to copy it so I could cut myself out, lift myself bodily out of this classroom where I'd been trapped for most of my life. It would be, I decided, a way of paying tribute at last to all the shadows not present here, a way of saying no to mere prettiness, to a view of reality that lied. And it would be, as well, a way of preparing myself to leave academia at last: this classroom as metaphor, as trap.

But now I've changed my mind. As I continue this year to appren-

But there is a different kind of performance at the heart of the renascence of poetry as an oral art—the art of the griot, performed in alliance with music and dance, to evoke and catalyze a community or communities against passivity and victimization, to recall people to their spiritual and historic sources.
—Adrienne Rich

All of us on life's journey should strive to live the symbolic life.
—C. G. Jung

tice myself to my dreams, moving more certainly into my own depths, I consider the possibility that what I've been given here, in story and photograph, is a mirror. What might I see if I chose not to remove myself but to look more closely? What if this first-grade classroom were indeed an image for a kind of necessary apprenticeship, a lifetime's discipline still at its earliest, first-grade stage?

What would I see?

The path leads down to what has been forgotten, ignored, repressed, shut out. This is a first-class passage to the great below: the trapdoor opens onto darkness. And though the soul balances on her own thin threads, pleading for protection at the threshold, it is time not for flight but for the journey down. The ways of the underworld are perfect. The terrible mother will turn her back, will cast upon you the eye of death, drawing from you those first infant cries born out of the dark. It is all new to you, and strange, hearing this voice cry out from your own shadows. This is the first taste. She knows you now, even in daylight, by the trail you leave behind. She claims you as hers.

This photograph of my first-grade class is not of a lie but of an early promise. Both mothers, my Muses, are present here—Crow Mother standing beside me, and the Lady of the Flowers, who reaps abundance and has sent her gifts—the goddesses of death and life. Butterfly, pinned to the wall, opens her bountiful wings. I am a child of the mothers. Their flowers spring to life, the gift of hands. I say yes to this service. I am hers.

I have, at this writing, left academia after teaching for twenty-five years. It was surprisingly easy, like lifting myself bodily out of a photograph I've simply and surely outgrown. At one level, academia was indeed a trap, a place I stayed in too long because I believed it fostered real learning. It took me a long time to understand that, as an institution, academia serves the fathers, perpetuates ways of knowing that disconnect us from the sources of life. The direction I'm headed in now is still a mystery. I talk about it as moving in harmony with the Tao, creating space for the mothers, shaping my life from the inside. Healing is here, and poetry, those double blooms in transformation's gorgeous display. At times, because my identity was so connected with the academic world, thinking about leaving made my hands sweat, as though I'd be leaping off into space, like a circus acrobat performing for the first time without a net. But now I have new images: of self in soul-school walking the

Everything is gestation and then bringing forth. To let each impression and each germ of a feeling come to completion wholly in itself, in the dark, in the inexpressible, the unconscious, beyond the reach of one's own intelligence, and await with deep humility and patience the birth-hour of a new clarity: that alone is living the artist's life—in understanding as in creating.
—Rainer Maria Rilke

highwire with her balance pole—the pole that's at once hook, line, and sinker—fishing the mothers' waters for memories, mirrors, messages. For poetry. All the shining detritus of the Great Below.

Bio

Karen Elias earned her Ph.D. in Mythology and Women's Studies from the Union Graduate School and taught at the college level for more than twenty-five years. She is now on the lookout for new ways to teach. This time, she wants the beauty she loves to be what she does. So far, it's been poetry in all its many guises—writing; working with women in prison; doing arts education; fighting to keep Lock Haven, Pennsylvania, safe from incineration; and learning the healing arts of Reiki and hypnotherapy. Her next dream is to help create a school where we might learn to walk in beauty.

William F. Farnan

In 1983 I was a moderately successful graphic artist. As a change of pace from two-dimensional representation, I enrolled in a class titled Sculpting the Figure in Clay. At the first session I was faced with a reclining model and a lump of clay. The instructor told me to just go at it. I picked up a piece of clay, manipulated it, and experienced a physical response close to passion. My life changed.

My pursuit of knowledge and determination to develop my skills in figurative sculpture was focused and intense. When I needed to give more attention to developing myself as a sculptor, I withheld attention from my profitable pursuits in the graphic arts. My income declined as my passion for sculpture increased. At some point, I realized that I had crossed a threshold. Not only was I taking sculpture seriously, but sculpture was taking me seriously. We had a relationship . . . a very demanding relationship.

When I work with clay something special happens to me. My body feels the gesture of the figure I am modeling. My face feels the expression of the face I am trying to capture. My sense of ego is limited to anger at my stupidity or frustration with my lack of skill. Often I am surprised at the results of my efforts, as they seem beyond my skill. At times I say "Thank you" to an invisible someone for helping me produce a decent sculpture.

The fact is that I have a committed relationship with something outside myself and a responsibility to put my best effort into that relationship and create what it demands. When I started learning to sculpt I felt as though I had a sensual relationship with a very passionate and strong primitive female force. I hoped to make this alluring force mine. I did not realize that there was a good possibility that she would make me hers. At present, my passion for the primitive female force still burns, but my hopes to subdue her have vanished. I do her bidding. It is the work that I take seriously rather than myself.

The work comes to the artist and says, "Here I am, serve me." The artist must be obedient to the work.
—Madeleine L'Engle

The eye with which I see God is the same eye with which God sees me.
—Meister Eckhart

One of the pleasant parts of being an artist is exercising the imagi- nation. One of the unpleasant parts is dealing with money and financial responsibilities. The imagination is a wonderful support when financial disaster comes through my door. I look at the sculptures in my studio, calculate their selling prices and, presto, my financial dilemma is solved! At other times I imagine that the phone will ring and someone will be offering me a commission. This fantasy has become real on many occasions.

Several years ago I was in financial *extremis* at Christmas time. The phone rang. It was a man who had purchased a cast of a bust I had sculpted of St. Thomas More. He wanted to order a bronze cast and inquired about the possibility of my sculpting a four-foot statue of the saint to be mounted in a niche on the second story of St. Thomas More School. I made a model of the statue and gave him an estimate for production. He paid me in advance. Christmas was great that year. The statue was unveiled at a special mass and still stands in that second- story niche. It does seem that if I am dedicated, hardworking, and loyal to my Muse, things work out. They do not work out the way I wish sometimes, but they work out.

I lack the genius and youth to be a great sculptor. Great sculptors stand on the shoulders of good sculptors and good sculptors stand on the shoulders of competent sculptors. Being accepted into the fellowship of sculptors is a big deal to me. Being dedicated to the work is an honor. When the work is going well and sales are good, the difficulties of producing an honest piece of work and keeping the wolf away from the door seem trivial. When the work does not go well and the wolf comes through the door, I have my magic weapon . . . my imagination.

The only joy in the world is to begin.
—Cesare Pavese

Art is food. You can't eat it but it feeds you.
—Bread and Puppet Theater Manifesto

Bio

Bill Farnan was born in Brooklyn, New York and attended the Art Students League, the American Art School, and the School of Visual Arts. He also studied design at New York University. He holds a B.A. from Manhattan College and a Ph.D. from St. Louis University. Since

1968, he has been a professional artist specializing in calligraphy, manuscript illumination, graphics, and sculpture.

Eryk Hanut

For Maria Todisco and Bridget Bell

I haven't any fixed memories or childhood reminiscences about wanting to be a photographer or writer. I'm convinced that there are, at least, two categories of artists—those who are called very early to a vocation and who have what amounts to an obligation to do something with their hands; and a second group, the one to which I belong, who discover by a tortuous and winding path—almost by luck—an activity they never thought about and that proclaims itself the center of their life.

Marlene Dietrich used to say to me, "Cezanne was Cezanne because he couldn't do anything else." She was right. After a certain period, whose length is as variable as human character, the thing that has to furnish your existence imposes itself on you, like the most violent manifestation of passion. I had an old woman friend in France who was a nurse until age seventy. Then, after retiring, she was possessed by an almost sexual craze for painting. She painted all the time, not well, really, but with fire. Everything that came near her, old papers, the obverses of envelopes, kleenex, found itself daubed gaudily with oil paint or covered with sketches. The last time I saw her—she died in her sleep two months later—she told me, out of breath and as if illumined by magical joy, "I have just seen Van Gogh's *Irises*. I am going to change my style!"

Personally, I don't believe that an artist has a "vision." There is a global vision which surrounds us all, into which we enter sometimes. But this vision is universal and is graced to us from time to time; it does not belong to us. Sometimes I have the impression that I become a little the things I am photographing—but the things I am photographing do not become *me*. Every form of art or creativity, I think more and more, is the invocation of a superior force that comes and lives in us for a while. This

The only Zen you find on the top of the mountains is the Zen you bring up there.
—Robert M. Pirsig

theory would explain the anguish of the white page that afflicts writers, or the afternoons spoiling canvas or film when nothing arrives. When she knew that she had performed below her talent and legend, Eleonora Duse would say, "This evening the gods did not come down."

I'm often asked what you should do to be a photographer; I am still at the state where I'm learning what *not* to do. The one certainty I do have is that you have to *look*, really *look*, at people and things. Apart from what I call "instantaneous flashes," which do not repeat themselves and which I take just as I receive them, as if photographic fire from heaven, or a ray of light that slips between two closing doors, photography is very meditative for me.

I observe my subjects—inanimate ones, for the most part—and I let them observe me. You can receive only what you have given; you must be attentive, because things in nature evolve at a much faster rate than we do. A pebble has just as intricate and mysterious a history as the most fascinating human life. The confrontation or exchange between photographer and subject takes a time that cannot be measured in human minutes. I simply *know* when I have to take the photo. I never know why. It is like obeying an interior order, or a signal, or a vital function. Basho, the Japanese Zen poet said, "Learn about a pine tree from a pine tree and about a bamboo stalk from a bamboo stalk. . . . The artist should detach his mind from self and enter wholly into the object, sharing its life and its feelings."

Having the most complex of cameras and studying in the most prestigious academies will not bring anything to the process of creation if you do not first possess the humility of looking. That is the first step towards any form of authentic expression. And you go on repeating that first step, tirelessly, until the end.

We must assume our existence as broadly as we in any way can; everything—even the unheard of—must be possible in it.
—Rainer Maria Rilke

To draw, you must close your eyes and sing.
—Pablo Picasso

Bio

Eryk Hanut was born in 1967 in Copenhagen. He grew up in Berlin, Brussels, and Paris. He is a photographer, writer, and set designer. His first book *I Wish You Love—Conversations with Marlene*

Dietrich (Frog, Ltd., 1996) is a memoir of his friendship with the great star. A frequent contributor to *Vogue, Elle,* and *Body Mind Spirit,* his photographic work has been exhibited all over the world.

Hanut lives with author Andrew Harvey in the desert of Nevada. Their two collaborations, *Light Upon Light* (North Atlantic Books, 1995) and *Mary's Vineyard* (Quest, 1996) are bestsellers. Their third collaboration, *Jesus, Son of Man* (Tarcher) will be released in spring, 1998.

Excerpt from

"The Wait"

The sight of the diner made Shadrack happy. It took him an hour to walk there and an hour to walk back, but it didn't matter. He felt like a pilgrim. When he was refused, it took everything to hold his anger in. He told his wife, Sadie, that he only accepted Jesus so he wouldn't have to kill nobody. "It is easier to murder than to love," Shadrack believed. He was following Dr. Martin Luther King, Jr. who was following Jesus. Love your neighbor as yourself. Turn the other cheek. We shall overcome.

He knew in his bones it wouldn't be long. The hush of the patrons when he came through the door rejuvenated him. He described it every time he could to Sadie and the civil rights workers. "They hearts don't even beat when they see me coming in here."

It didn't matter how much they stared. How the hate showed through their skin. When their mouths fell open and they dropped their forks, he knew he had them. They had to think about it, had to choke down their food. Shadrack relished being the most important thing at 12:00 every single work day. He even had the power to take that grin on Happy's face.

It wasn't that Happy didn't like Negroes. They had their place. They cooked good, and he had to admit that he liked their music, and when no one was looking he glimpsed with admiration the beauty of the colored women as they passed by his diner windows. Nothing wrong with it. He didn't mean nothing by it; he was just a man. It was so amazing to see how many colors and sizes black women came in. No matter. He just wasn't ready for it, this integration. None of the whites were. It wasn't *what God intended. Things is just fine the way they are. Happy told all the girls, "Just tell 'em no service. Don't try to make sense with them; you can't get through to these militant Negroes, so just tell them no and go. Hey I like that 'No and go!'"*

The silliness of it got a chuckle from the other poorly paid staff, but Dominion knew the weight was on her.

She gathered herself and walked to the table where Shadrack sat. She had to say it, but she made sure to stare just over his head. The last time she looked in his eyes, she stuttered, remembering Mr. Hank Jacoby, the colored man that used to tend Grandpa Dan's garden. Shadrack's graying hair took her back to old Hanky. He worked diligently but always had time to tell her tales about when he got together with God and run the devil outta heaven. Or the time when only he could lift up the house to get her brother Walter out from under it when he was born. She didn't realize that Old Hanky might just be stretching the truth until she found out he was born in 1912.

Shadrack wanted so much for this young white girl to look at him. She was a child of God just like him and maybe she would understand. He didn't really want to eat in this Happy Diner, just have the right to eat there if he wanted to. He preferred to eat the grits and eggs at Chappie's on his side of town where you could have salmon croquettes, Red Devil Hot Sauce on the table, and get a eye full watching the pretty brown skinned waitresses. He was a man, and should eat where he pleased.

Shirlene Holmes

"In the beginning, God created . . ." Genesis 1:1. Whenever I doubt myself as a writer, I always go back to the basic thought that God began her divine career as an artist. Every culture acknowledges that God was an artist first. The first divine act was to make, to create. So God is an artist, and so am I. I call myself an artist, and respect it as a God position, a very sacred and important vocation.

A woman is in her words.
—*African proverb*

I have been writing since the age of nine. Even at that time, I was caught up with language, fully aware of the power of words to charm, stun, tear asunder, and heal. I have spent hours studying and practicing just how to take the twenty-six letters of the alphabet and move them around so that people will be changed by what *I* have to say.

I consider myself a vessel, a channel, by which spirit travels and speaks at this time. I believe that each era has its artists for a specific reason. We are the ones who are charged to serve humanity, which is our community. We lift up the issues and ideas so that all will be corrected, educated, elevated, and empowered.

In order to meet my challenge as an artist who writes, I have become a good listener. I absorb life through my senses and record it. I am a deep thinker, analyzing, visualizing. I am affected by everything: music, other artists, sound, light, food, nature, animals, all things.

What has inspired me all my life is my love of my African-American culture. I am so proud to come from such a strong people. It is the language of the black church and neighborhood that has had the most profound affect on me. We are an amazing people, so diverse, so sensual, so explosive, so beautiful, so creative. We took our despair and with ingenuity, made art and survived. Our whole existence in this country has been one of great struggle and triumph. I draw from my folks when I write: how we talk, how we fight, how we love. Black soil is so rich.

I write from the multifaceted experience of being African-American and female. Often my work is informed by the compassion, anger, sorrow, and intensity that being a black woman gives me. I am very grateful for and privileged in this identity. I am sure that because I know and celebrate who I am, my writing reaches beyond the confines of my limited perspective.

I write because I cannot help it. The stories are always in my mind. I visualize characters and situations, most of which I do not get to write down. Only the precious few ever make it to print. I hear voices. I see people in my mind and plot how to tell others about them. I make stories, trusting that my readers and audiences will see themselves in them.

I choose the genre that best fits the story I want to tell. For immediacy, I write a play. For a story that needs space to explore, I write fiction. For an idea that must be condensed and said quickly, I write a poem.

I believe my writing is successful because I began as a poet. It was the best training. I savor language and want my readers and audiences to experience the words of my stories, not just the ideas of them. It is important that I say a thing I want to communicate in a way that can reach others. I strive to be unique, but at the same time speak in a familiar voice.

I write because I feel so deeply. Human suffering moves me. Emotions have power and I am constantly creating characters that must channel the power of their fear, love, anger, and so on. I try to make something from all the chaos and coldness of day-to-day life, something that will nourish us at this time.

I capture the voice of the marginalized in society. I am most interested in letting the story of the disenfranchised be heard. So I write about the oppressed: the transvestite in a small town, an Alabama blond-haired waitress having to say "No colored served here" even when it's against her conscience, two black lesbians in the 1890s who adopt a baby and name her Jesus. I write about the blue-collar workers, the African-American and Asian-American conflict.

These are people who interest me. I want to listen to them talk. I admire how they survive, how they go against the grain. I want to write their testimony.

I believe there is a little of me in every character I write. I believe

To believe in God for me is to feel that there is a God, not a dead one, or a stuffed one, but a living one, who with irresistible force urges us towards more loving.
—Vincent van Gogh

my poems, plays, and stories are my offspring, so these people I create or re-create must be a part of me. Perhaps they show my best side, the one that beats the odds, the one that speaks out, the one that dies with dignity.

I write to preserve the words that I hear around me. I write for the same reason the photographer snaps a picture, to hold a moment in time, so that it might be appreciated and studied. Although I do not write with detail, I always make sure to leave room for the reader or audience to join me in creating the story. I want them to fill in that which I have left out.

Although I write from the specificity of what I know—my experience and culture—I believe my work reaches the universal because it is about people and what they make of life.

In order to write well, I make myself available and vulnerable. I set a time to write; I choose as topics those subjects that might be taboo, embarrassing, uncomfortable. I test my works out on myself. Do they make me feel? I often write things that make me cry—and also laugh. To have the authenticity that I demand of my work, I make sure I am stirred by the piece before I free it for others to experience.

I believe that each of us is a part of God's kingdom, given the talent to do something for the greater good of humanity. When we do not fulfill our purpose, we are very unhappy and the world is deprived. I do what I do because it is part of the divine plan for my life and the lives of others who happen to read my work or see my dramas. I believe in a greater force that guides us all, not in accidents or coincidences. When someone is exposed to my work, it is by divine appointment; they are supposed to see it or hear it because there is something in it for them.

It is my duty as a writer to call attention to the people that most of us walk by every day, not noticing their profundity or their great connection to each of us. Whether we're conscious of it or not, when we look at the lowly, we find our kin. When we begin to love, respect, and appreciate our neighbor, we love ourselves.

It is my responsibility and privilege to be a creative writer in this time. I follow in a great tradition of black women writers who have accepted the challenge to record and create. What would we do without the words of Lorraine Hansberry, Zora Neale Hurston, Octavia Butler, Alice Walker, and Toni Morrison? They and many, many others are my teachers and inspiration.

Today before tomor-row.
—African proverb

Silence is also speech.
—African proverb

I do see myself as an activist, a revolutionary, and an ethnographer. When I open myself enough to write and tell the story truthfully as I know it, then I have done my part. I have put light in the world, and the whole purpose of art is to shine a light, to raise the consciousness of humanity. I cannot say exactly who I am writing for. I know I am writing literature I want to see on stage when I go to the theater and on the shelves when I go to bookstores. I want my readers and audiences to be as diverse and abundant as snowflakes. In addition, I want those who identify with the characters in my writing to be affirmed. I want to reach the world through my writing, and I want it to embrace me in return.

My greatest honor is that my work will outlive me. I want to write stories and poems and plays so profound that they will be able to save people today and in the millennium to come. This is an enormous challenge, but many, many writers before me have done it.

To achieve this goal, I must become more self-aware. Self-awareness is God-awareness. I must reveal light, releasing and letting go of all weight. I must study and ponder and practice the art and craft of writing daily. I must welcome discipline and criticism, and I must labor in confidence, not conceit. I must listen and I must be willing.

This is the advice I give to all artists, writers in particular.

Whatever you resist, persists.
—Robert Anthony

Bio

Shirlene Holmes is a nontraditional scholar whose major areas of interest and specialty are solo performance and playwriting. She also has expertise teaching African-American Studies. Along with scripting for the stage, she is both a performer and storyteller.

Holmes, an associate professor of communication at Georgia State University in Atlanta, earned her B.A. in English from York College of the City University of New York, her M.F.A. in theater, and her doctorate in speech from Southern Illinois University in Carbondale.

Her play, *A Lady and A Woman,* which was a finalist in the national Jane Chambers Play Competition (1992), was recently remounted at Emory University (September 1995) and will be published this year by Applause Books.

Holmes' recent achievements include a residency at the Mount Sequoyah New Play Retreat. She was one of the artist/scholars featured in *Theatre Insights Journal,* and her solo biographical drama, *Conversation With a Diva,* was produced by Actors Theatre of Washington (February/March 1996).

Sister Paula Matthew, CSJ

I began sculpting when I was eighteen years old. I was starting the spiritual journey, wanting to know what this process of life was all about, wanting to know what it was like to grow up. I had always painted, but at the age of eighteen, I developed an allergy to oil paint and had to give it up. When I would begin to draw, I would see five lines instead of the one I had drawn on the paper. I thought I was having eyesight problems! I didn't know this reaction was part of the allergy. My father sent me a shoe box with a four-by-four-by-twelve piece of hemlock in it and a set of Exacto carving tools. His note read: "Honey, all the lines in the world are in this block of wood. Go find them. This is your teacher." When I was done with the block, it was a tiny piece of wood. That's how much the "teacher" taught me before I could get a form out of it.

After that, I carved something that looked like a woman holding out both hands. I realized that what had emerged while I was carving was a part of myself. It was a surprise when I finished. I knew it was me with my hands open, and I said, "All right, I will be open to all of the lines, but I request one thing: I wish to carve the Divine's face all over the world."

That was the beginning of my sculpting. I continued to carve and let the wood be the teacher. In the process, I let go of any goals I had for the finished piece. I simply had a relationship with the material, letting the wood and life teach me as I touched them.

I have found that my spirituality is formed when I let go, begin to work, and go into the process of creating. For me, art has been like this: I have a deep question within me and I would love to know the answer. It's like working a koan in Zen. I cogitate on a root question. I wonder about spirituality. What is a spiritual path? Or I wonder about the nature of death. What does the face of death look like? In the process of creating a piece about the root question, I let the wood itself teach me, let the wood

Lift the stone and you will find me; Cleave the wood and I am there.
—Jesus

answer the question. When the piece is finished, I view it anew, study the answer that emerged in the process of creating. Years later, I can return to view a piece and still learn more about the answer to the root question, the answer that came from and through the process of creating.

If we allow it, the arts can talk to us. It's as if the Spirit or the Source speaks through us, allowing us to touch an aspect of the Divine. It's like having a talk with God. At the end, you look at the piece that has been created and wonder how it happened. At least for me, it happens like this every time I let go into the process. I've come to trust the process, to surrender control and let myself be surprised by the outcome. But for some, that kind of surrender is frightening.

We're so afraid of explorations in art. Ask most people about making art and they'll say: "I can't do it." We've missed something. We let our egos and our whole being get tied up in the product instead of letting the process surprise us. We're so afraid of how the end product will be judged that we lose our ability to allow it to arise through the creative mode of the art itself.

Art is very subversive because it can change a person in its process. Art pushed me to let go more and more; it pushed me to the farthest limits, to let go of all control. When I say to myself that I have no techniques, and just go into the process, that's scary. It was very frightening to work with that first piece of hemlock when I was eighteen. It was death dealing to my ego and control mechanisms.

For me, the tool, the wood, speaks to me. When I'm carving, I wonder what's emerging. My mind wants to control the process and say, "*This* should be emerging." When I say that, I'm up against the wall of myself and my own control mechanisms. I only get my own answer returned with nothing solved. But when I say "No" to my desire to control the outcome, the teacher is right there in front of me constantly, within the wood itself. The challenge is learning to trust, to let go into the creative process of my Self. When I do that, the Divine speaks to me through the very soul and cells of my body. Through that interplay between my body and the wood, a unique expression occurs.

I believe that the works that touch the Divine or teach us or are still with us centuries after their creation are the ones that did not come out of a place of power or control or technique but came at the moment when the heart let go and God answered the question.

When you gain knowledge of anything else, you gain knowledge of some thing; when you gain knowledge of spirit, you become knowingness itself. All questions cease because you find yourself in the world of reality, where everything simply IS.
—Deepak Chopra

Bio

Sister Paula Matthew, CSJ, is a visionary artist whose major works of art are being shown in The Gallery, Windsor, New York. Symbolism is the foundation upon which Paula creates. She sees in symbol and her art reflects that seeing in wood, stone, and paper. She believes that through symbol we can experience more than one level of reality.

Paula acknowledges Divinity as the prime artist from which all art arises and springs forth and the one who speaks in multiple ways. "Art is the consciousness that exists between the creation and the one viewing the creation. It is that magical middle ground that opens a window on eternity."

It is for this reason that Paula does not sign any of her carvings. Instead a gemstone is imbedded in the sculpture to symbolize that mystery which happens between the viewer and the art. In this way, Paula honors the artistic process in each of us and believes that the piece will evoke what is needed for each one's journey at the moment.

Excerpts from

"Pillars of Salt"

From "The Wife of Lot"

Of course, I looked back, wouldn't you? How else can the story be told?

From "The Laughter of Sarah"

I'm not the one who's barren around here, Abraham. Hagar's child was not yours either. The child promised to you will have to be made by someone else. Perhaps by God himself. Now doesn't that make you laugh? When Hagar went away, you thought it was jealousy, a man's only explanation for what divides one woman from another. Not jealousy, Abraham. I loved Hagar like a sister. I insisted she tell you that Ishmael was not your child and she refused. Well, I don't blame her. You would not have been amused.

The point is, Abraham, do I have to spell it out for you? Even if I had been your sister and not your wife, I didn't want to be bartered with the Egyptians for your safety. To be given by my own husband—by you—to another man so you could sleep soundly at home in your tent. What kind of people are you, you chosen men of Israel? Was the god of Abraham barren when he conceived of you?"

From "The Song of Miriam"

Moses wanted me to dance for death, for victory. For the Egyptians sinking and screaming under walls of rushing water. For the whinnying horses and the choking men. To shake my tambourines for death! "You'll lead the women, Miriam," he said to me. I refused.

Who is this god that *celebrates* death? That sings for the destruction of the enemy? That tricks the victims? Each house in Egypt had already lost a firstborn, and now the best of the Pharaoh's officers were drowned. The deep waters covered them; they sank to the depths like a stone. And we, the women of Israel, mourned with the women of Egypt. We suffered their sorrow with them. And I did not shake my tambourines. And I did not dance. And the women kept the silence with me. We heard the cries come up out of Egypt. And we could not rejoice. The men under Moses caroused all the night long. But we women kept watch, rocking our children in sorrow.

The second time I questioned Moses it was easier. The text says I murmured against Moses. But I didn't murmur. I shouted. There's always another side to the story.

And I said to Moses, "One day we women will have a *chosen* land, not one that has been promised. A Sanctuary. A Place of Refuge. Where war will be no more and force will not be used against us. Where lies will not be told about us and circumcision will not be the mark of the select. Where the altar will be open to us, and our daughters shall rejoice, and dance for life, not death. Where accusations will not rise against us and those we love will be of our own choosing. Where our attackers will be rendered impotent. Where we will walk with men of mercy who seek justice and the way of right. A land where we will walk with those who know the sorrow and the song. I, Miriam, Prophetess and Singer, tell you it is so. Let the women go."

Eunice Scarfe

I grew up in a world governed by religion, a religion brought from Norway in the worn trunks of my ancestors, a pietistic Bible-based tradition that created enclosure— enclosure that governed thought, action, feeling, sexuality, spirituality, belief, behavior—and ignored the creative place of the imagination. Nothing was untouched by the law of the fathers. Everything was prescribed. We were born in sin, we recited every Sunday, and nothing could save us except the blood of the lamb.

It made no sense to me. Born in sin? Blood? Of a lamb? I asked questions and got no answers—none that I could understand, that is. I soon understood that I was at fault for trying to understand. I wept through my first religion class in the church college, a college where a brave professor had added systematic theology to the syllabus of a required course. I cried because of the comfort of hearing words that made sense. Of being in a place where questions could be asked. Of speaking about the function of religion in general rather than about the precepts of a religion in particular.

There was order in thought, I decided, an order that endowed thinking with beauty. For a long time I thought that 'the peace that passes all understanding' would be found in knowing. In understanding everything. In making sense of the world. I was wrong.

The experience of creation of any kind was foreign to me, and for escape I turned to intellectual pursuits, away from the faith of the fathers, though also perhaps toward. Wasn't I by heritage a Lutheran, descendant of Luther and the Norwegian Hauge whose questions radically altered the shape of religious practice in their time? I took all the theology and philosophy courses offered and continued on at graduate school in English at a university where I intended to audit everything offered at the divinity school. If I could just make sense of everything, I would be at peace. Or so I thought. I slipped in and out of depression, hardly aware

Any story told twice is a fiction.
—Grace Paley

To write is to admit.
—Kristjana Gunnars

of its force, certainly not of its cause. And so I finished a graduate degree at the University of Chicago, married, went to England, and in time came to Canada where my husband took a position at the University of Alberta and we started a family.

The summer I turned thirty-nine I started to write, like a bomb exploding. I signed up for a creative writing class at the university. I began a novel told in short stories, stories narrated by the youngest daughters in two families, children of a musician and a clergyman. The stories were true to the emotion of my experience, but entirely invented.

In the writing of these fictions, I found a place where emotion and thought, feeling and memory, the known and the unknown, could live together in harmony. I found a process so comforting, so true, so powerful, and so whole and holy that I could not and would not stop. I found that the music of my childhood became the controlling metaphor of the collection, that the complex implications of "love your neighbor" were addressed in every story, that the metaphors of the religious texts of my childhood gave me a rich resource for understanding metaphor in my writing, and that the rhythms of the scripture—those poetic and powerful lines—invaded every page I wrote. I found that I hadn't so much abandoned the religious tradition, as reentered it through the world of the imagination.

I wanted to re-create for the reader the emotional, spiritual, and intellectual distress of the questioning child in a world of absolutes. A world in which intuition and imagination were dangerous. A world in which sexuality and spirituality—yes, spirituality—were controlled. A world in which paradox was painfully present—the paradox of living where one thing was preached and another was practiced, where "love your neighbor" was prescribed and "judge your neighbor" was lived. The distress of the children in these stories was inner. The difficulty I faced was how to dramatize that internal anguish. The first story I wrote put a young girl inside an evangelical rally. She begs to "go forward," and when she does, she is molested by the adult assigned to pray with her. It was an image for everything that was to follow: the harm done by the hands of those whose primary responsibility was to protect.

It never occurred to me to write my story in the form of memoir. Was not memoir only for the accomplished and famous to write, and then at the end of their lives? The mask of fiction was a natural form

You write and while you write you are ashamed for everyone must think you are a crazy one and yet you write and you know you will be laughed at or pitied by everyone and you are not very certain and you go on writing. Then someone says "yes" to it and never again can you have completely such a feeling of being afraid and ashamed that you had when you were writing and not any one had said "yes" about the thing.
—Gertrude Stein

for me, a mask behind which I the writer could hide. Hadn't I hidden in silence all through my childhood, watching, listening, wondering, aching? I took to the mask of fiction like a duck to water and taught myself to write by reading the words of the women writers that lined my shelves. I wrote with one hand on the keyboard and one hand turning the pages of their books. How to structure a story? Where to begin? How to find language to fit the lives of girls and women? How to show, not tell, the story I knew? How to let the story tell itself?

Writing for me became a dance between the writer and the elements of story. I wrote primarily to engage in this dance and not particularly for the sake of reaching an audience. Or rather I wrote in order to invite the reader into the dance, to have a reader say, "Your story made me want to write mine," or "Your story made me remember my own." That is the best kind of response from the reader.

In the entry into the world of imagination, from which all story springs, I believe that we come closest to the world of the spirit, and hence all making of story becomes a spiritual place. It is a place of the most intense solitude but also a place where the most intimate communal experience can be achieved: that of sharing story. Story is a place where meaning can be made and remembered. And story is also the creation of vision: balancing what was with what might have been. Balancing what is with what could be. Balancing dark against light. Balancing joy and sorrow. Kim Chernin says that the "spiritual means sensitivity to an unseen order. It means, further, the capacity to take seriously one's relations to this unseen order, so that one can be transformed by it." In making story, I take seriously the unseen order. As writer, I am transformed in the making of story; the reader is transformed in the reading of story.

When my husband died in 1988, I was finishing my first collection of stories. I stopped writing completely. How could I continue in the face of his death, particularly a senseless death caused by an impaired driver? It was a long time before I continued writing. And when I did, I believe I was governed by the understanding that story is the sole place where I could experience the eternal. Story precedes us and will outlive us. In story is the resurrection of the dead. In the time we are here, we can, if we choose, contribute to the making of story. Or we can keep silent. For myself, I choose not to keep silent. Writing doesn't depend on inspiration

> *When the writing starts, listen.*
> —*Marianne Moore*

> */To write is to /locate my own address inside my head.*
> —*E. M. Broner*

or education or talent. Writing depends on choice. It is an act. It is both the most freeing and the most demanding task you can undertake.

As Willa Cather says, "Artistic growth is, more than anything else, a refining of the sense of truthfulness. The stupid believe that to be truthful is easy; only the artist knows how difficult it is."

Like many other new writers, I was afraid that my first story would be my last. I discovered, as have many others, that when the first work is finding its completion, another story edges its way forward, often born from the first. While I was finishing the collection called *Sorrow, Sing Sorrow,* I found myself looking back at the images of women who appeared in the Old Testament. In the absence of voice for these women in the original text, I invented voice and found speech for their stories. The wife of Lot spoke first: "Of course I looked back, wouldn't you? How else can the story be told?" Others followed—Sarah, Tamar, Jephthah's daughter, Diana—until I had a collection of seven, the last of which was Miriam, in whom I invested all of my understanding and vision of a woman of strength and courage and power. This collection is now called *Pillars of Salt*. If we as women chose to write nothing other than the stories of silenced or invisible women in myth, history, literature, and family, we would have work to last us all our lives. I am now working on several texts at once, moving back and forth between them. One is set in ancient Egypt, one in Norway, one in northern Alberta. There is no end to story.

Two years after my husband died, I began teaching writing for the Women's Program at the University of Alberta. I wanted to surround myself with the chorus of story. I wanted a place where imagination and creation were protected and allowed. I needed the sound and comfort of women's words. And I asked, How can I help a woman find and fill her own blank page *in her own voice?* How can we become the subjects of our own texts, having for so many centuries been the objects of the texts of others? Instead of assigning finished stories for class evaluation, I ask them to bring a blank page. We do first drafts together, working in solitude but not alone, gathering fragments of story written in short segments. We listen to each other's voices and often hear echoes of our own stories in the words of another. And then we elaborate or extend or insert these fragments into a text of our own. All text is story, no matter what we call it—prose, poetry, memoir, journal—all partake of story,

You don't have anything if you don't have the stories.
—Leslie Marmon Silko

---

and each writer works in whatever form she chooses. I never tire of hearing women's voices in my classes. Each is like one voice in a chorus, different in tone but always in harmony.

I often find women in my classes who are carrying the weight of an untold story. Sometimes they are not even sure what it is. I always say that the place and the time, the page and the power, may have been absent before. But now is the time, now you must begin to admit and allow. Set the story free. Let it seek its own form and shape. The making of story requires exercising the muscle of creation, and with each page the muscle becomes stronger. Writing, among all its various faces, is a way of keeping fit in body, mind, and soul.

For me, writing is a way of life; it's what I do. It's where I see the darkness and where I celebrate the light. It is where I am most alone and most connected. If I were to choose a color for the role of writing in my life, it would be red: red for vibrancy and blood and joy and richness and fire. No one can take it from me, and no one can retire or fire me from this work of mine. It's who I am: a writer. It's what I do: I write. It's where I meet the community I am most connected to: other makers of the written word.

Only one thing is more frightening than speaking your truth. And that is not speaking.
—Naomi Wolf

Bio

Eunice Scarfe was born in Fargo, North Dakota, in 1944 and now lives in Edmonton, Alberta with her two daughters, Sarah and Emily. She attended high school in Seattle, college in Minnesota, and graduate school at the University of Chicago and the University of Alberta. Her short stories have been published by Room of One's Own, Matrix, *Malahat Review,* NeWest Press, Fifth House, Prentice Hall, Coteau, and General Press, among others. She is a recent winner of the Prism International Short Fiction prize and a 1996 finalist in the *Malahat Review* novella competition. Since 1990 she has taught writing for the Women's Program at the Faculty of Extension, University of Alberta, where she is currently Writer in Residence. Her Writing Adrift Seminars for Women have been taught coast to coast, from Washington, D.C. to the Yukon.

Tammy Tarbell-Boehning

When I was young, even though we were full-blooded Mohawks, we lived close to, but never on, the reservation. My territory was the middle ground between two cultures. Because of the prejudice against Natives, I struggled to stay in the white world and never felt accepted by the Native people. I began to deny my heritage and created a false Caucasian identity for myself.

I had many secrets to harbor as a little girl and turned to art as a refuge, drawing out my feelings in picture after picture that no one understood but me and the Creator. Drawing was my only way of expressing my sadness at trying to live this lie, and I put all my secrets and all my prayers into these works of art. But the pain and isolation never went away, and I turned to alcohol for the escape that it offered.

I struggled with alcoholism for many years while still using art as a means of expression, pouring my secrets into every piece. I was suicidal and thought that the only way I could stop what I was doing was to die. I didn't realize that I could stop it and live, that living could be an uphill climb, and that I could get up and away from the terrible things I was doing and feeling.

It wasn't until I was thirty years old that I decided to sober up and make a commitment to my art. As hard as I worked on sobriety, I worked at finding out who I was under the lie, under the illusions I had been creating for so many years. I was diagnosed with a chemical imbalance and treated with medication that helped to balance my system. It was as though a cloud lifted and I had the ability to see for the first time. And once I could see, I could start the long, hard journey of letting go of my old self and my old behaviors.

I was working in clay at Syracuse University, and for the first time I saw my artwork as a vehicle for my survival. At first I was doing blackware pots, putting my prayers and secrets into each one, the way I did as a child. The work was solitary and between me and the Creator. But there came a time I needed to speak out. I wanted someone else to know what went into these pots. I wanted someone to know my secrets. I started to speak and accept who I was and to work on the dolls which symbolized the spiritual aspects of women. Images of women from different roles started rolling in—clan mother, faith keeper, dancer. I was beginning to feel pride in my Native heritage and accept myself as a Native woman. Great joy came when I was able to admit to myself that I was Native and that I was worthwhile. I had a gift to share and I wanted to share it.

I had to go through a process of emptying myself out, for I was no longer able to blame my past or my family for the state I was in. I had to drop the illusion that I was white. I had to admit that it was OK to be imperfect, and part of being perfect was being white.

In getting rid of what doesn't belong and filling myself up with my own thoughts and feelings, I am being responsible for who I am. I am letting go of the prejudice and racism from both cultures, letting go of the world where I could not accept myself and had to put on a facade to survive. I have come to realize that my people accepted me all along and that it was me who couldn't accept myself.

As far as my ability to create, I know it comes from a higher source. When I first hooked up to the Creator, I was in the midst of a hurricane. My whole life, my whole being and its meaning, was in chaos and there was only one spot deep in the center that caught my eye, so I centered on that. I thought if this is what I think it is—my soul, my connection to the Creator—then if I nourish it and nurture it, it will grow and I'll remain connected to the higher source. That was my linkup.

I try to stay connected, to stay mindful of that, but it is a struggle. I am so busy trying to make a living that I have little time for the creative process. Lately, I have burned myself out churning out piece after piece of the same thing in order to support my family. I've not had the time to let the voice rise up from inside. I've not had the time to dwell on my ideas, to be in touch with my higher power. I know this is something that needs to be changed, and as I write this now I am committing to reclaiming that time for myself.

I need time for the new ideas to come in, time for my creativity to express itself. These dolls have something deep to say to me and I need to give them time. If I'm focused on money, then I'm out of focus. My biggest struggle is to stop and take a look at what's going on inside and to find the courage to let that out.

For me there's like a spot inside, something deep inside gnawing at me, wanting to come out. I want to be able to pull it out in my work so someone else can take a look at it. My work is like a question to them, "Is it there inside you, too?" If it is, they'll feel this thing in my art and we'll connect on some level. They'll know what I'm doing, and something about this connection is healing. That commonness between us starts a chain reaction—what they find in my work, they take with them where they go and share it with another and another. It happens in a way you can't describe, but it happens and every artist knows what it feels like when it does.

But that spot has dimmed now and I need healing again. I need to reach out and ask for what I need so this feeling of dying, this feeling that the light is going out, will disappear. For me, the light only comes through when I'm sharing with others; if I isolate myself, I start to become self-centered, and that self-centeredness leads to depression and lack of creativity.

Some days I have to force myself to keep at it. I keep doing it because I know I have to. Even though I can't imagine the whole piece, I have to keep working on the first part, knowing that the next step will show itself to me in time. Some days I am only able to write my ideas down or to sketch them in a pad, and these are very big steps, giant steps, a way of saying I want to do this, I'm going to do this, and I will be ready when the time comes.

Bio

Tammy Tarbell-Boehning has been a self-employed potter and sculptor since 1980. She has recently completed a year-long internship at the Iroquois Indian Museum in Howes Caves, New York, where she worked and demonstrated hand-building and wheel-throwing pottery techniques to the public. She received the Native American Woman

Achievements Award in 1996 and was the first woman to receive the Award of Excellence from the Iroquois Indian Museum. Her sculptures have received first-place awards in Oklahoma City's Red Earth Indian Market, the Eitlejorg Museum in Indianapolis, the Gallup Ceremonial in New Mexico, and at several exhibitions throughout the Northeast.

A graduate of Syracuse University, Tammy has taught at the Community Folk Art Gallery, Onondaga Community College, and Metropolitan School for the Arts.

Cris Williamson and Tret Fure

Jan Phillips: When you write your music, who is your audience?

Cris: I am writing to the world. Women respond deeply to my music because they are looking for something that they find there, but it's a mysterious "something" because it's not about gender. If you carefully look at my lyrics, you see that it's a universal viewpoint, a bird's-eye view of the human condition. I write about all the aspects of the human condition that interest me and cause me to ponder. We [women] are considered emotional beings who live in an interior world, and perhaps it's that interior world of the poet that strikes such a chord with women. Women have always responded deeply to poetic sensibility, but it's not to say that men cannot. It's easier for women to talk to women about it—because you're talking to "yourself" and that's a joy. That's the greatest joy of having women as our audience because they know about this stuff—but so do the men who come, so they're a joy to talk to, too.

We go from the personal through the general into the universal, as good writing should. Writing, if it stays only in the personal, turns out to be not very interesting; it is pretty much self-indulgent unless in this very personal realm it manages to extend into the universal, like a good photograph. When we went to Russia we sang in English but people were moved by our music because it's universal.

Tret: I always considered myself a folk artist. Then I got into new wave and punk, but I was always working in music, either performing or engineering. I fell into the women's community through playing with Cris, and I am ever grateful because it's a very rich audience.

They're there for you and are very supportive. When I write, I write for myself and the world.

JP: What daily rituals keep you centered and focused?

Cris: I enjoy morning time for myself, drinking coffee and reading. I pull ideas for writing from whatever I read and always have my writing books close at hand. Chance furthers the prepared mind, and if you're prepared, you're always ready should the Muse come knocking. A part of my mind is always awake and dreaming at the same time. Good humor and good health always help the creative process. There's no time for reflection on the road, and it's a lot harder to write because there's no cushion for us. We do everything ourselves. We don't travel in a big bus, don't have tour support, no roadies to help us. We do all of it, bear all of it ourselves. The ritual is our daily life of getting up and doing the thing, and we stay cheerful with each other. It's very hard work but because we have each other, it really helps to balance that out.

Tret: I try to do yoga every day to calm myself and prepare myself. I don't read much or watch TV, but I enjoy myself in the studio, at my computer, in my garden. We're trying to take this year off to write, and since we've been home we've been writing lots of songs. That kind of time is a real luxury, but we have to tour so much to support ourselves; that's the main ritual.

Cris: I take care of the horses. Being with them calms my heart and my mind. If you're calm you can write whenever you have an idea, and we can write songs in two hours sometimes. We're having a ton of fun writing together and have a real muscularity about our skills now after honing them for the past thirty-some years. We've started to teach, and we're learning more all the time as we practice the same things we teach others.

There are lots of different styles, lots of different teachers, and lots of different ways. People just need to figure out what their tools are—if they like to write better on word processor or with a number-two pencil on a yellow page.

JP: How do you define success?

Cris: I've always felt successful. I think it's a sense of wholeness, that you are exactly who you are at all times no matter what it is you're doing. If I'm out there working with the horses, I'm the same person who's on stage, just lit in a different way. I'm expressing myself in a slightly different way, but at the core of it is the same believable person. I think that when you believe in yourself and are believable to others, you are successful.

I don't define success in terms of wealth, other than inner wealth, because a lot of people are rich whom I don't consider successful at all—they can't extend themselves to others, they can't communicate. There are all kinds of wealth, all kinds of definitions of success, and I'm a self-defined success. Some days I don't feel quite so successful, so skilled. Like athletes—they run the same race every day. Sometimes they run it really well and sometimes they trip and fall. And so it is with musicians and mothers and photographers and whatever it is you do in life. There'll be days you don't feel so successful, but you should have an overall view of yourself as a work in progress. Success should be looked at from that perspective: constantly defining yourself, constantly working to be a whole human being, to be effective and give back more than you take.

Tret: To me, success is the ability to do the work I want to do, the work I really love. Even when I didn't have a recording deal, I was able to work at engineering to support myself in my art, and that is what success means to me. I have longings sometimes—for a tour bus or a record label, road managers, people who would tune and hand me the guitar for each song. That's very appealing and I wish we had that level of support, but I don't think I'd feel more successful. I'd just have a little more time on my hands.

When I toured alone, it didn't matter if I was singing to thirty or three hundred people. I always had a great response to the show and that's what gave me a chill and sent me home every night feeling high. To me, that's success too.

Cris: When you go to sleep at night, when you can say to yourself no matter how many people were there, no matter how much money you made or didn't make, you did your very best, you gave all that you could give and never less—that's success.

JP: What inspires you?

Cris: It could be the smallest thing, from a little bird sitting on a wire in the most perfect way opening up his beak and letting out this liquid stuff called song, and I say "Boy, maybe one day I'll get to be that good!" Or it could be the sun coming up in a fine way, or the way light falls on something, or the smell of good cooking, or watching other artists do what they do.

I'm inspired by people who do difficult work in the world; who save children; who, instead of being wealthy, choose to be a doctor in a small town; who try to keep nuclear war at bay; who go into prisons and bring education there; who go into the dark places of the world and shed a little light, which is a lot. We're inspired by so much, and that's because we're awake. You've got to open up your eyes to see it, and then you can be inspired by the smallest, the least of these things.

Tret: I'm inspired by other people's music and by the fun I have in my own studio, creating new work. Ideas come out of the vacuum, out of the heavens. I don't have a lot of tools for my writing, but it comes easily and off the top of my head. I'm inspired by my life, my love for Cris, my gardening, watching my seeds turn into beautiful plants. And when my mother died, her death, as difficult as it was, was a great source of inspiration. Somehow I was able to take that grief and torment and turn it into songs of healing. It's been a great gift to be able to do that.

So many women have come up to me who identify with that song and thank me for allowing them to grieve and talk about the subject we don't talk about much. Talking about my grief has opened doors for them. That's an amazing thing when your own music can touch people so greatly. That's what art is—true art is able to move people beyond themselves.

Cris: . . . or into themselves. In my case, I feel that I've moved people within themselves in an almost magical way. I always write for myself first, to feel better. I don't sit down and say, "I'm going to write a healing song," because I think that that would show too much intent, and the intent would dissolve the result. It would be too visible. Mostly what I do is write because I'm feeling lonely, feeling sad, feeling empty, and so I seek some way to fill myself up again. Images of water, earth, air, and fire come up, and people respond to these images because they are basic to all cultures.

I was given a gift of this voice and my job is to sing, to express those tones. There are certain tones that climb inside each human life and work like little keys in doors that people think are firmly and permanently locked. And they unlock so easily through sound; they unlock so beautifully through music and words. If you do it right and sing it right every night, there could be a life that's changed out there.

Like a great watering hole, we're all about "welcome"—everyone is welcome to drink as long as there's water. There will be times when each artist has to hang a sign: "The well is being cleaned. Do not drink now."

As an Aquarian, I'm a water bearer; my job is to pour water all over everybody, into every ear. Music is food and medicine. It's not something to put you to sleep—it's to wake you up—and the dreams we spin are dreams to wake you up.

Bio

CRIS WILLIAMSON

Since the mid-seventies, Cris Williamson has been one of the most successful artists in independent music. She has sold out Carnegie Hall, performed in most major concert halls in the United States, and sold nearly one million albums. Cris has come to be known as one of the pioneers of women's music, an ambassador of positive female imaging through music that celebrates human strength, tenacity, and the resilience of women.

Cris started her musical career at the age of sixteen, recording her first three albums while still in high school. She helped create Olivia Records, an independent women-owned company, which recorded fourteen of her albums. She has taken her music to Australia, Europe, and Russia. Most recently, she has brought her skills to teaching song writing around the country. At forty-nine, Cris has seventeen albums to her credit along with a coveted Parents' Choice Award for her enchanting sci-fantasy musical, *Lumiere*. She is cofounder of In the Best Interests of the Children, Inc., a wholly volunteer nonprofit pediatric AIDS organization that develops entertainment-based HIV education programs and cosponsors Camp Colors, the family day camp for kids with HIV/AIDS, with Lasell College in Newton, Massachusetts. Most recently Cris has started her own record company, Wolf Moon Records, with her partner Tret Fure and is currently producing a new release.

Discography

Artistry of Cris Williamson, The World Around Cris Williamson, Cris Williamson, The Changer and the Changed, Live Dream, Strange Paradise, Meg and Cris at Carnegie Hall, Lumiere, Blue Rider, Prairie Fire, Snow Angel, Portrait, Wolf Moon, Country Blessed, The Best of Cris Williamson, Circle of Friends, Postcards from Paradise

TRET FURE

Tret Fure is as much at home performing music as she is behind a recording console. She has built a reputation as both engineer and producer, and has a number of albums, including seven by Cris Williamson, one by June Millington, and three of her own, to her credit. She has worked as mixing engineer for several projects on Fabulous Records, the soundtrack for the miniseries *Palmerstown USA*, the PBS documentary *Is Anyone Home on the Range?*, and music for several movies.

Tret's first album, *Tret Fure*, was recorded in 1973. She toured extensively following its release, opening for such acts as the J. Geils Band, Yes, and Poco. In 1975 she went behind the scenes and received on-the-job training to become one of the first women engineers in Los Angeles. She spent the next five years honing her skills as an engineer and producer, then returned to the music scene in 1980 to tour with June Millington. Tret connected with Cris Williamson in 1981, and they have been touring together ever since. They are currently at work on an album to be released under their new label, Wolf Moon Records. She is cofounder with Cris of In The Best Interests of the Children, Inc.

Discography

Tret Fure, Terminal Hold, Edges of the Heart, Time Turns the Moon, Postcards from Paradise.

Works Cited

Anderson, Margaret. *The Fiery Mountains*. New York: Horizon Press, 1970.

Bell, Roseann, Bettye Parker, Beverly Guy-Sheftell, eds. *Sturdy Black Bridges*. Garden City, N.Y.: Anchor Press/Doubleday, 1979.

Bender, Sheila. *Writing Personal Essays: How to Shape Your Life Experiences for the Page*. Cincinnati: Writer's Digest Books, 1995.

Cahill, Susan, ed. *Writing Women's Lives—An Anthology of Autobiographical Narratives by 20th Century American Women Writers*. New York: HarperCollins, 1994.

Campbell, Joseph. *Hero with a Thousand Faces*. Princeton, N.J.: Princeton University Press, 1968.

_____. *Myths to Live By*. New York: Viking Penguin, 1972.

Castaneda, Carlos. "Does This Path Have Heart?" *New Age Magazine*, March, 1994.

Cather, Willa. *Song of the Lark*. Boston: Houghton Mifflin, 1988.

Chardin, Teilhard de. *Divine Milieu*. New York: Harper Collins, 1975.

Christ, Carol. *Diving Deep and Surfacing—Women Writers on Spiritual Quest*. New York: Beacon Press, 1995.

DeCrow, Karen. *Sexist Justice*. New York: Random House, 1974.

Forster, E. M. *Passage to India*. New York: Harcourt Brace, 1952.

Fox, Matthew. *Original Blessing*. Santa Fe, N.M.: Bear and Co., 1983.

Gardner, Howard. *Creating Minds—An Anatomy of Creativity Seen Through the Lives of Freud, Einstein, Picasso, Stravinsky, Eliot, Graham, and Gandhi*. New York: Basic Press, 1993.

Gilbert, Sandra and Susan Gunbar. *No Man's Land—The Place of the Woman Writer in the Twentieth Century*. New Haven: Yale University Press, 1988.

Goldberg, Natalie. *Wild Mind—Living the Writer's Life*. New York: Bantam, 1990.

_____. *Writing Down the Bones—Freeing the Writer Within*. East Lansing, Mich.: Shambhala Publications, 1986.

Goodwin, Gail. *The Finishing School*. New York: Viking Press, 1995.

Graham, Martha. *Blood Memory*. New York: Simon and Schuster, 1992.

Griffiths, Bede. *Return to the Centre*. Springfield, Ill.: Templegate Publications, 1976.

Hall, Manly P. *Questions and Answers: Fundamentals of the Esoteric Sciences*. Los Angeles: Philosophical Research Society, 1978.

Hamilton, Edith. *The Greek Way*. New York: W. W. Norton, 1958.

Hanh, Thich Nhat. *Peace Is Every Step*. New York: Bantam Doubleday Dell, 1992.

Heilbrun, Carolyn. *Writing a Woman's Life*. New York: W. W. Norton, 1995.

Heyward, Carter. *Touching Our Strength*. San Francisco: HarperSanFrancisco, 1989.

Hillesum, Etty. *An Interrupted Life: The Diaries of Etty Hillesum*. New York: Simon and Schuster/Washington Square Press, 1991.

hooks, bell. *Outlaw Culture—Resisting Representation*. New York: Routledge, 1994.

Houston, Jean. "Calling Our Spirits Home." *Noetic Sciences Review,* Winter 1994.

Jong, Erica. *Fear of Flying*. New York: Doubleday, 1994.

Jung, C. G. *The Spirit in Man, Art and Literature*. London: Routledge and K. Paul, 1966.

Kandinsky, Wassily. *Concerning the Spiritual in Art*. New York: Dover Publications, 1977.

Kent, Corita and Jon Steward. *Learning by Heart: Teachings to Free the Creative Spirit*. New York: Bantam, 1992.

Keyes, Ken, Jr. *The Hundredth Monkey*. 2d ed. Coos Bay, Oreg.: Love Line Books, 1982.

Lamott, Anne. *Bird by Bird—Instructions on Writing and Life*. New York: Doubleday, 1995.

LeGuin, Ursula. *The Left Hand of Darkness*. New York: Harper and Row, 1980.

L'Engle, Madeleine. *Walking on Water—Reflections on Faith and Art*. New York: Farrar, Strauss, Giroux, 1995.

Leonard, George. *Transformation—A Guide to the Inevitable Changes in Humankind*. Los Angeles: J. P. Tarcher, 1987.

Lorde, Audre. *Sister Outsider: Essays and Speeches*. Freedom, Calif.: Crossing Press, 1984.

Lessing, Doris. *A Small Personal Voice*. New York: Knopf, 1974.

Levertov, Denise. *The Poet in the World*. New York: New Directions, 1973.

Mairs, Nancy. *Voice Lessons*. Boston: Beacon Press, 1994.

Mansfield, Katherine. *Journal of Katherine Mansfield*. New York: Ecco Press, 1983.

Merton, Thomas. *No Man Is an Island*. New York: Harcourt Brace, 1955.

Metzger, Deena. *Writing for Your Life*. San Francisco: HarperSanFrancisco, 1992.

Moore, Thomas. *Care of the Soul*. New York: HarperCollins, 1992.

Moraga, Cherrie, and Gloria Anzaldua, eds. *This Bridge Called My Back—Writings by Radical Women of Color*. Watertown, Mass.: Persephone Press, 1981.

Munro, Eleanor. *Originals—American Women Artists*. New York: Simon and Schuster, 1979.

Nevelson, Louise. *Dawns and Dusk—Taped Conversations with Diana MacKown*. New York: Scribner, 1976.

Nin, Anaïs. *Diary of Anaïs Nin*. New York: Harcourt Brace Jovanovich, 1966.

Norman, Marsha. *The Fortune Teller*. New York: Random House, 1987.

Olson, Tillie. *Silences*. New York: Dell, 1979.

Osbon, Diane K., ed. *Reflections on the Art of Living—A Joseph Campbell Companion*. San Francisco: HarperCollins, 1995.

Palmer, Helen. *The Enneagram: Understanding Yourself and the Others in Your Life*. San Francisco: HarperSanFrancisco, 1991.

Paterson, Katherine. *The Spying Heart*. New York: E. P. Dutton/Lodestar Books, 1989.

Phillips, Jan. *Making Peace: One Woman's Journey Around the World*. New York: Friendship Press, 1990.

Potok, Chaim. *Book of Lights*. New York: Knopf, 1981.

Priestly, J. B. *Literature and Western Man*. New York: Harper, 1963.

Reuther, Rosemary Radford. *Disputed Questions: On Being a Christian*. Nashville: Abingdon, 1982.

Rich, Adrienne. *What Is Found There—Notebooks on Poetry and Politics*. New York: W. W. Norton, 1993.

Rilke, Rainer Maria. *Letters to a Young Poet*. New York: Random House, 1986.

Rinpoche, Sogyal. *The Tibetan Book of Living and Dying*. New York: HarperCollins, 1992.

Roberts, Jane. *The Individual and the Nature of Mass Events*. Englewood Cliffs, N.J.: Prentice-Hall, 1981.

Roosevelt, Eleanor. *You Learn by Living*. Louisville, Ky.: Westminster John Knox, 1983.

Sarton, May. *Sarton Selected*. New York: W. W. Norton, 1991.

_____. *Mrs. Stevens Hears the Mermaid's Singing*. New York: W. W. Norton, 1993.

_____. *Journal of a Solitude*. New York: W. W. Norton, 1973.

Sewell, Marilyn. *Cries of the Spirit*. Boston: Beacon Press, 1991.

Starhawk. *The Spiral Dance*. New York: Harper and Row, 1979.

Steinem, Gloria. *Outrageous Acts and Everyday Rebellions*. New York: Holt, Rinehart and Winston, 1983.

Stravinsky, Igor. *Memories and Commentaries*. Berkeley: UCLA Press, 1981.

Weil, Simone. *Gravity and Grace*. New York: Putnam, 1952.

Wolkstein, Diane and Samuel Noah Kramer. *Inanna Queen of Heaven and Earth—Her Stories and Hymns from Sumer*. New York: Harper and Row, 1983.

Woolf, Virginia. *The Moment and Other Essays*. Orlando, Fla.: Harcourt Brace, 1948.

_____. *A Room of One's Own*. New York: Harcourt Brace, 1989.

QUEST BOOKS
are published by
The Theosophical Society in America,
Wheaton, Illinois 60189-0270,
a branch of a world organization
dedicated to the promotion of the unity of
humanity and the encouragement of the study of
religion, philosophy, and science, to the end that
we may better understand ourselves and our place in
the universe. The Society stands for complete
freedom of individual search and belief.
For further information about its activities,
write, call 1-800-669-1571, or consult its Web page:
http://www.theosophical.org

*The Theosophical Publishing House
is aided by the generous support of
THE KERN FOUNDATION,
a trust established by Herbert A. Kern
and dedicated to Theosophical education.*